DESIGNING RESIDENTIAL WILDERNESS PROGRAMS FOR ADULTS

The Professional Practices in Adult Education and Lifelong Learning Series explores issues and concerns of practitioners who work in the broad range of settings in adult and continuing education and lifelong learning.

The books provide information and strategies on how to make practice more effective for professionals and those they serve. They are written from a practical viewpoint and provide a forum for instructors, administrators, policy makers, counselors, trainers, instructional designers, and other related professionals. The series contains single author or coauthored books only and does not include edited volumes.

Sharan B. Merriam
Ronald M. Cervero
Series Editors

DESIGNING RESIDENTIAL WILDERNESS PROGRAMS FOR ADULTS

Michael J. Day
and
Ellen M. Petrick

KRIEGER PUBLISHING COMPANY
MALABAR, FLORIDA
2006

Original Edition 2006

Printed and Published by
KRIEGER PUBLISHING COMPANY
KRIEGER DRIVE
MALABAR, FLORIDA 32950

FROM A DECLARATION OF PRINCIPLES JOINTLY ADOPTED BY A COM-
MITTEE OF THE AMERICAN BAR ASSOCIATION AND A COMMITTEE OF
PUBLISHERS:

This publication is designed to provide accurate and authoritative information in
regard to the subject matter covered. It is sold with the understanding that the
publisher is not engaged in rendering legal, accounting, or other professional service.
If legal advice or other expert assistance is required, the services of a competent
professional person should be sought.

Library of Congress Cataloging-in-Publication Data

Day, Michael J., 1946–
    Designing residential wilderness programs for adults / Michael J. Day
and Ellen Petrick.
        p.   cm. — (Professional practices in adult education and lifelong
        learning series)
    Includes bibliographical references and index.
    ISBN 1-57524-261-3 (alk. paper)—ISBN 1-57524-282-6 (pbk. : alk.
paper)
    1. Outdoor education. 2. Adult education. I. Petrick, Ellen, 1960–
II. Title. III. Series.

LB1047 .D38 2006
371.3'85—dc22   2005044978

10   9   8   7   6   5   4   3   2

Dedicated to Henry David Thoreau for reminding us to live each day courageously and to Edward O. Wilson for contributions to science that never lose sight of mystery and magic

FIELD GUIDE INTRODUCTION

Something mysterious, unpredictable and exciting often results from time spent in settings little touched by the ubiquitous
hand of human beings—time spent in wild places. The size of
these wild places can range anywhere from the pristine lands
covering most of the state of Alaska to a patch of wildflowers
in a city park. Though we often live in close proximity to such
places, we tend to establish only slight relationships with them.
One of the main themes addressed in this book is how adult
residential education programs, when located in wilderness settings, can dramatically strengthen these relationships to the mutual benefit of the individual and the planet. At a time when
research and experience acknowledge the physical and emotional benefits of frequent encounters with wilderness, wilderness remains at risk, and our technological society makes it ever
easier to function in isolation from the natural world.

This book is also written to acknowledge another relationship individuals can develop when participating in adult residential education programs. This is the relationship with the child
who resides within each of us. Some child-like behaviors are released quite naturally in a residence environment while others
need to be redeveloped, such as keen observation of surroundings, alert senses, life lived fully in the present, and unquench-
able curiosity. Reconnecting to these characteristics is a major
component of the programs we design and describe in the pages
that follow. Many of the illustrations in the book come directly
from the authors' work in wilderness settings but the underpinning assumptions and programmatic techniques may be applied in a variety of general education or personal renewal endeavors. At its heart, this work is about revitalizing the human

spirit, especially with regard to relationships—with others, with the child within, and with wilderness.

The chapters that follow reflect the impact of two powerful 20th century social movements in the United States. The first, beginning in the 1920s, was the adult education movement. Due to ever-increasing amounts of leisure time, discussion ensued as to ways more and more adults might engage in both individual and social improvement. The other was the wilderness movement of the 1960s and early 1970s. Resulting from a fusion of politics, science and vision about the value of wildness, this movement forged new management policies favoring natural regulation and the preservation of natural conditions.

Through sensitivity, commitment and opportunity, these two social movements provided a framework for redefining relationships to the natural world. These efforts also lead to creative ways to strengthen bonds between people and wilderness. This book is written to support the efforts of both educators and individuals seeking new ways to connect with the natural world.

Michael and Ellen have been in the business of providing residential education in wilderness settings for over 20 years. Each brings a unique perspective and a wealth of experience to this effort. Their experience encompasses audiences both young and old, spans coast to coast, and has occurred within the realms of academia, natural resource agencies, and non-profit organizations.

CONTENTS

PREFACE

We met for the first time in Yellowstone National Park in the fall of 2000. Sensing we shared similar interests, a mutual friend introduced us. We did have a lot in common. For example, we enjoyed spending time outdoors, especially in Yellowstone, and we were both experienced residence educators: as a university professor, Michael organized his first weeklong adult residential program in 1996; Ellen, as Yellowstone's Education Program Manager, organized her first youth residence program in 1994. We had both witnessed again and again the transforming effect of residence life especially when experienced in wilderness settings. We were also convinced that the long-term protection of places like Yellowstone depended upon increasing its base of support. We both embraced the motto, "In the end, we conserve only what we love. We love only what we understand. We understand only what we are taught" (Baba Dioum, Senegalese ecologist).

The initial meeting went well. We developed and then delivered the first of many adult residential education programs in Yellowstone in the fall of 2002. Over the years we learned a great deal from our work together. When we met, we were both successful residence educators struggling with institutional/ agency formalities—content expectations, constraints, and accountability. From the beginning of our collaboration Michael was less concerned with specific course content than he was with the mere fact of providing a residential experience for graduate students in a new wilderness setting, though some of his university colleagues questioned the educational value of such programs. He spoke comfortably and unapologetically about other ways of learning, personal growth and community building—

things that can be readily accessed through residential learning. As a Yellowstone Park employee, Ellen found this way of thinking peculiar. Having a rich background in biology and environmental studies, science content came naturally to her. Ellen's major challenges had become procuring grants and quantitatively measuring the success of her programs.

As our collaboration evolved, we found that Ellen needed to think less like an administrator chasing grants and more like someone who believed in magic, and Michael needed to stop justifying residential learning programming to university colleagues and administrators, and accept the unique opportunities such programs provided. We began looking more holistically at what residential programs could achieve. In addition, since we both enjoyed hiking, watching wildlife, and geyser gazing, we still needed opportunities to spend more time in Yellowstone. So began our shared work in crafting residential education experiences for adults in wilderness areas.

Something mysterious, unpredictable, and exciting often results from time spent in settings little touched by the ubiquitous hand of human beings—time spent in wild places. The size of these wild places can range anywhere from the pristine lands covering most of the state of Alaska to a patch of wildflowers in a city park. Though we often live in close proximity to such places, we tend to establish only slight relationships with them. One of the main themes addressed in this book is how adult residential education programs, when located in wilderness settings, can dramatically strengthen these relationships. At a time when research and experience acknowledge the physical and emotional benefits from frequent encounters with wilderness, adult educators are continually challenged to find ways to fortify the bond between students and their natural environment. This book is written to support these efforts.

This book is also written to acknowledge another relationship individuals can develop when participating in adult residential education programs. This is the relationship with the child who resides within each of us. Some child-like behaviors are released quite naturally in a residence environment while others need to be redeveloped, such as keen observation of surround-ings, alert senses, life lived fully in the present, and unquench-able curiosity. Reconnecting to these characteristics is a major component of the programs we design and describe in the pages that follow. Many of the illustrations in the book come directly from our work in wilderness settings but the underpinning as-sumptions and programmatic techniques may be applied in a variety of education endeavors.

Pragmatically, those in general adult education or wilder-ness education, as well as residential education teachers and pro-gram organizers all may find many practical applications in the material covered in this book. Philosophically, the same practi-tioners may find the values underlying the programming appeal-ing and meaningful, professionally as well as personally. At its heart, this work is about revitalizing the human spirit, especially with regard to relationships—with others, with the child within, and with wilderness.

The last major publication in the United States to address adult residential education appeared in 1971 in Cyril Houle's *Residential Continuing Education.* Its focus was university-based residential education. Since that time there have been only a sprinkling of publications, most notably Jean Fleming's 1996 doctoral dissertation, *Participant Perceptions of Residential Learn-ing.* To date, few works are available to assist planners in the design and delivery of residence programs, and nowhere have we found a discussion of the relationship between such pro-grams and wilderness.

The book is organized into seven chapters. Chapter 1 in-troduces a rationale for conducting adult residential education programming in wilderness areas. It also provides a general con-text for the design of such programs, stressing the natural bond that exists between people and wilderness.

Chapters 2, 3, and 4 are the primary how-to sections of the book and are aimed at practitioners already engaged in or con-sidering adult residential education in wilderness areas. Chapter 2 explores pre-event issues such as forming a planning commit-tee and defining its makeup and role, creating a vision, deciding upon a program, finding a location and facility, selecting speakers and materials, attending to meals and logistics, determining fees, and marketing the program.

Chapter 3 focuses on running a residential education program. Issues examined include orientation, introductions and climate setting, community building, guidelines for organizing daily activities, suggestions for program presenters, and conducting the wrap-up session. Special attention is given to strategies for facilitating learning and making the program meaningful as well as enjoyable.

Chapter 4 focuses on post-event activities such as debriefing instructors, writing thank you notes, constructing and sharing group photo/scrapbook/memento materials, conducting follow-ups, and completing a final evaluation.

Chapters 5 and 6 are written for a broader audience—program planners as well as the general educator—and cover suggestions for helping program participants more fully experience wilderness surroundings. Chapter 5 is devoted to sauntering. Techniques are presented to facilitate active exploration and openness to novelty and discovery in natural environments. Chapter 6 is devoted to a powerful reflective and recording tool, that of journaling.

"Final Thoughts," Chapter 7, revisits major themes introduced in the text with special attention to components of adult residential education in wilderness areas that easily transfer to and are applicable to everyday life. It also explores the overall value of designing adult residential education programs in wilderness areas.

Three appendixes are also included. In Appendix A is a sample of a preliminary program advertisement. Appendix B includes a sample of packet materials mailed to participants a few months prior to a program: welcome letter, agenda, and clothing and equipment list. Appendix C is a sample program evaluation form.

ACKNOWLEDGMENTS

Many people deserve recognition and thanks for helping with this book. A special thanks to Mary Roberts at Krieger Publishing for encouraging us to share our residence experiences and take on this project. Because we hoped the perspectives and suggestions covered in these pages would appeal to a broad audience, numerous students and colleagues were consulted. To University of Wyoming graduate students Laurie Bedford, Matt Caires, Tony Czech, Kristi Frush, Kalpana Muetz, and Lee Nabb, we thank you for reading early drafts of the book and for all your thoughtful observations. To University of Wyoming colleagues Mick and Pam Clark we greatly appreciate your thorough examination of the text and your many useful comments, and thank you, John Kambutu, for your enthusiasm for the project and for your interest in establishing similar residence programs in Kenya. We are also extremely appreciative of the interest in the project by national park educators Roger Anderson, Chief of Cultural Resources for Yellowstone National Park, and Jenny Golding, Program Manager for the Yellowstone Association Institute, whose viewpoints limited the jargon and stretched our thinking. A special thanks also to Brenda Schussman, who first introduced us to the form of journaling we use—her creativity and expertise are clearly reflected here and gratefully acknowledged. We are especially grateful for the interest and support of Jean Fleming whose research and writings on adult residence education guided us throughout the project. Though we fully acknowledge and credit all our reviewers with much that may be useful in the book we hold none responsible for its shortcomings—for that we take full responsibility.

Finally, we very much thank our families—Susan, Steve, Ben and Tom—for their support, patience, and encouragement, especially for having to share some of "their" time with the project.

THE AUTHORS

Michael Day is currently associate dean and professor of adult education in the College of Education at the University of Wyoming. From 1982 to 2001, except when he chaired the UW Division of Lifelong Learning and Instruction, he headed the graduate program in adult and post secondary education at the University of Wyoming. Day is also a past chair of the faculty senate, recipient of three UW teaching awards, and a frequent contributor to professional development programs sponsored by the UW Center for Teaching Excellence.

Day began his adult education career as a University of Maryland extension student in 1970 in Wiesbaden, West Germany. In 1972 he became an academic field coordinator for the University of Maryland (European Division) and completed both his bachelor's and master's degree through overseas programs delivered to members of the U.S. Armed Forces community in Germany. From 1972 to 1977 he held various adult education positions from ESL/GED instructor to field registrar coordinator and trainer. He received his Ph.D. in education from the University of Michigan in 1981.

Day's major teaching and scholarship interests are in learning communities, historical and philosophical foundations of adult education practice, and adult residential education in wilderness areas. He is a past president of the Wyoming Adult Education Association, cofounder and director of the Wyoming Adult Education Social Action Theater, and an experienced residential education coordinator. Day is also a wilderness adventurer and photographer (visit www.michaeldayphotography/ to share in some of his journeys). Day and his wife Susan live in Laramie, Wyoming, where they enjoy numerous outdoor activities such as running, hiking, skiing, and kayaking. They are frequent national park adventurers.

Ellen Petrick was the National Park Service's Program Manager for Formal Education in Yellowstone National Park from 1994 to 2001. She oversaw a number of the park's gateway and regional outreach programs including *Expedition: Yellowstone!*, a residential program for school groups based out of the Lamar Valley, and the park's Junior Ranger Program that serves over 15,000 children each year.

Petrick received her undergraduate degree in biology from Tufts University in 1982. She worked as a graduate teaching fellow at the New Jersey School of Conservation for a year after which she received a master's degree in environmental education in 1984 from Montclair State College. Petrick has worked as a seasonal park ranger for the Park Service and has done contract work in education for the U.S. Forest Service, Utah's Division of Wildlife Resources, the Museum of the Rockies in Bozeman, Montana, and the Weber State Museum of Natural Science in Ogden, Utah. She also worked as a cross-country ski instructor at Weber State University and as a teacher-naturalist and education program director at the Ogden Nature Center.

Petrick grew up in Yorktown Heights, New York. She began spending summers in Yellowstone as a college student. Petrick is currently living in Klamath Falls, Oregon, where she is working to establish the Klamath Outdoor Science School. She will soon be returning to live and work in Yellowstone.

CHAPTER 1

Wilderness, the Child Within, and Residence

To the extent that each person can feel like a naturalist, the old excitement of the untrammeled world will be regained. I offer this as a formula of re-enchantment to invigorate poetry and myth: mysterious and little known organisms live within walking distance of where you sit. Splendor awaits in minute proportions. (Wilson, 1984, p. 139)

When the two of us think about adult residential education in wilderness areas, we think primarily about the relationship between participants and wilderness and how both benefit from time spent together. For participants, residential living, almost in and of itself, has a transforming effect. Physically and emotionally removed from everyday responsibilities, a childlike sense of freedom results permitting participants to examine and even reevaluate their lives, their values, and their relationships. For wilderness, when participants accept that they are part of a complex and intimately connected web of life, they are much more likely to respect and preserve all remaining wilderness areas. Link residential living to wilderness, and the opportunity to contrast natural and civilized environments dramatically facilitates relationship building and self-examination. When program planners aim to reacquaint participants with the natural world, wilderness provides a powerful location for instruction—much more so than classrooms on a university campus.

The bond between people and wilderness is strengthened and enhanced when individuals gather in a residence program to examine specific themes and topics. It seems, therefore, fundamental that three things occur almost simultaneously when designing and delivering residence programs:

1. Experience and knowledge pertaining to a specific natural environment

2. Opportunity to interact with others

3. Time for individual reflection

Chapters 2, 3, and 4 cover how we design residence programs to achieve these goals. In this chapter we focus on the wilderness-individual relationship. First, we discuss the meaning of wilderness and its significance for contemporary societies. Next, we discuss adult education and examine courage, which we define as firmness of mind and will, as an appropriate outcome for adult education practice. Then we introduce one popular author/educator from the 19th century whose position on courage as a life goal still resonates with modern audiences: Henry David Thoreau. We conclude by providing a brief introduction to residential education and by connecting some of Thoreau's wisdom to adult residential education programs in and near wilderness areas.

WILDERNESS

What is wilderness? Nomadic people living prior to the development of agriculture and permanent dwellings had no need for the concept of wilderness. It was an agrarian lifestyle that delineated between cultivated and wild land. The word *wilderness* comes from the Old English *wil(d)deornes*, meaning wild or savage. To a pastoral and urban-minded people, this referred to untamed vastness: the darkest forests, the forbidding peaks, the barren deserts, and the uncharted seas. These were the realms of wild beasts.

The idea of wilderness has been defined differently by various cultures. In *Wilderness and the American Mind* (2001), historian and environmentalist Roderick Frazier Nash traced how the concept of wilderness evolved in the United States during the past 300 years from a place to be feared and viewed as an impediment to progress, to a place revered by romantics and nationalists, to a place to be both enjoyed and protected.

European conquest of their "new world" established the concept of wilderness as frontier waiting to be settled. The 19th century was a time of rapid westward expansion in the United States accompanied by wanton destruction and waste. Passenger pigeons and bison were slaughtered by the millions for sheer sport. Further, the Industrial Revolution drew increasing numbers of people away from the land; country life was infused with nostalgia. Without industry standards both people and the environment suffered. By 1890, wilderness had become a scarce resource at risk of being eliminated, and suddenly worth saving. American environmentalism was born from a new conservation ethic preached by 19th century prophets Henry David Thoreau, John Muir, and others. They argued wilderness had essential value for humankind.

Defining Wilderness

Today, both operational and legal definitions of wilderness exist. The Leopold Institute (n.d.), a federal research group, includes numerous views of wilderness in its definition:

> Wilderness can refer to lands designated or managed for the purpose of preserving natural conditions; for providing opportunities for solitude or primitive and unconfined recreation; and for their scientific, educational, scenic, cultural, and historic values. Wilderness can also refer more broadly to conditions offering personal opportunities for challenge, escape, or spiritual growth.

A legal definition of wilderness was provided by The *United States Federal Wilderness Act of 1964*:

> A wilderness, in contrast with those areas where man and his own works dominate the landscape, is hereby recognized as an area where the earth and its community of life are untrammeled by man, where man himself is a visitor who does not remain. An area of wilderness is further defined to mean—an area of under-

developed Federal land retaining its primeval character and influence, without permanent improvements or human habitation, which is protected and managed so as to preserve its natural conditions and which (1) generally appears to have been affected primarily by the forces of nature, with the imprint of man's work substantially unnoticeable; (2) has outstanding opportunities for solitude or a primitive and unconfined type of recreation; (3) has at least five thousand acres of land or is of sufficient size as to make practicable its preservation and use in an unimpaired condition; and (4) may also contain ecological, geological, or other features of scientific, educational, scenic, or historical value.

Building upon these two definitions, we define wilderness as a location where natural conditions are preserved—places, for example, set aside and protected in national parks and forests. Within these locations, ample resources are available to provide opportunities for solitude and renewal. In addition, these places are rich depositories of educational, aesthetic, and cultural values. We also refer to wilderness as a place where attitudes and behaviors differ from those of "civilized" living and offer numerous opportunities for self-reflection and growth.

Wilderness Today

The world's largest remaining wildernesses include the rainforests of the Amazon, the Congo, and New Guinea; the coniferous forests of northern North America and Eurasia; and the earth's deserts, polar regions and open seas (Wilson, 2002). Yet very few places, if any, are truly untrammeled by humans. Many scientists agree that as greenhouse gases cause global temperatures to rise, large-scale wildfires become the norm. Currently, sections of the earth's land surface are burned every year, sending plumes of nitrous oxide into the atmosphere. Glaciers and forests retreat up mountain slopes. As human populations continue to grow worldwide, terrestrial environments are losing most of their largest mammals, birds, and reptiles, upsetting the balance of interdependent animal and plant populations. The invasion of alien species into already stressed habitats further diminishes native plants and animals, often to the point of near collapse, forcing humans to intervene.

Many adults continue to treat wilderness as a commodity to be exploited rather than a resource to be cherished. As visionary conservationist Aldo Leopold lamented in the foreword to *A Sand County Almanac* (1949/1968):

> Conservation is getting nowhere because it is incompatible with our Abrahamic concept of land. We abuse land because we regard it as a commodity belonging to us. When we see land as a community to which we belong, we may begin to use it with love and respect. There is no other way for land to survive the impact of mechanized man, nor for us to reap from it the esthetic harvest it is capable, under science, of contributing to culture. (p. viii)

Suggesting that moral values should govern the relationship between human beings and the environment, Leopold preached an ethic where land was loved and respected. Wilderness does need supporters—supporters like The Wilderness Society, formed in 1935. Acknowledging the many challenges pertaining to wilderness preservation, our residence programs strongly promote stewardship and responsibility for wild places. For more information about The Wilderness Society (n.d.), visit its webpage.

Despite these realities, wilderness continues to exist, even to thrive in the unlikeliest of places. In fact, scientists are discovering new wildernesses all the time. The microorganisms of Yellowstone National Park's hot springs are a prime example. Currently, these microorganisms are attracting as much scientific attention as Yellowstone's bison, elk, and grizzlies. An enzyme from a microscopic organism discovered in one of Yellowstone's 10,000 thermal features led to the development of the PCR process (polymerase chain reaction), which made the study of DNA possible. Without PCR, there would not be the widespread use of DNA fingerprinting to identify criminals, DNA medical diagnosis, DNA-based studies of nature, and genetic engineering. Since this propitious discovery in 1966, microbiologists have flocked to Yellowstone's hot pools, hoping to discover beneficial applications for the uncommon, heat-stable proteins produced by heat-loving life forms (thermophiles) that thrive there. Researchers estimate more than 99 percent of the species living in Yellowstone's hydrothermal features have yet to be identified. In addition to thermophiles, Yellowstone's pools also provide homes for acid-loving organisms (acidophiles) that flourish at the very bottom of the pH scale in the park's hot sulfur springs. To read more about the microorganisms of Yellowstone hot springs refer to Brock (1994).

From the floor of the Mariana Trench to the tip of Mt. Everest, living organisms inhabit virtually every square inch of the earth's surface, and reside within it as well. Scientists have only begun to explore these little-known wildernesses. Educators could make great use of them.

Throughout this book, we repeatedly tout the value of time spent in wilderness for renewal and growth. People do need wilderness. But wilderness also needs people. Educators are encouraged to accept personal responsibility for this fact. Appreciation and understanding for wilderness of every scale must be purposefully taught. Programs designed specifically to teach about natural systems in natural environments are most effective at capturing hearts and minds—the surest route to a global land ethic.

MEANING, GROWTH, AND ADULT EDUCATION

As in the case of defining wilderness, adult education as a concept evolved over time and is difficult to pin down. Adult education authors Sharan Merriam and Ralph Brockett (1997) admitted that "defining adult education is akin to the proverbial elephant being described by five blind men: it depends on where you are standing and how you experience the phenomenon" (p. 3). What is known is that the term is primarily a product of the 20th century, popularized in the mid-1920s by the American Association for Adult Education, AAAE. (To read more about the AAAE and the early years of the adult education movement in the United States refer to Day, 1981, and Knowles, 1962/1977.) By the early 1960s, theorist and author Malcolm Knowles, who was once a member of the AAAE, concluded that the reason the term *adult education* was vague and confusing was because it suggested three meanings: (1) the process of learning once formal schooling is completed, (2) activities sponsored by agencies and institutions, and (3) a movement or field of study (1962/1977, p. viii). Self-directed learning, as when adults choose to read a book primarily for personal growth, Knowles acknowledged, was as much a form of adult education as the enrichment courses sponsored by a local community college. He also acknowledged that adult education as a field or a movement sprang from common or shared goals and values. Within this last usage of the term, much can be identified to guide the design and delivery of adult education.

It is not our purpose to identify and discuss the variety of values steering the work of adult educators. We do suggest, though, that a way of thinking about adult education was developed in the late 1920s suggesting that its purpose was more than satisfying utilitarian ends. AAAE members as diverse in core beliefs as Everett Dean Martin and Eduard Lindeman agreed that adult education began when formal education concluded and that its ultimate purpose was to add meaning to life. Whether through the path of reading and discussing "great" books (as promoted by Martin) or through addressing and solving societal issues (as promoted by Lindeman), adult education was encouraged primarily as a vehicle for renewal and growth. Lindeman wrote in 1926 that adult education "begins where vocational education leaves off. Its purpose is to put meaning into the whole of life" (p. 5). Martin (1926) espoused that at its core adult education was "the kind of education which sets the mind free from the servitude of the crowd and from vulgar self-interests" (p.viii). For both Lindeman and Martin, the ultimate goal of adult education transcended the acquisition of utilitarian skills.

We bring this up because the residence programs discussed in this book, though rich in content, are primarily designed to add meaning to life. These programs provide opportunities for adults to learn new things while stressing relationships, values, and beliefs. We believe our primary role as adult educators is to help learners feel better about themselves and their abilities and to nurture a desire to learn and grow throughout life. In addition, we fully recognize that learning and growth often require fundamental changes in behaviors and attitudes, and this requires courage.

For many adults, it takes courage to critically confront well-established patterns of behavior and beliefs. It takes courage to address complacency. It takes courage to confront fears, some of which may be associated with wild places. It takes courage to examine relationships with social groups as well as with other species.

As program planners, we recognize how fundamental courage is to growth, especially in regard to the individual-wilderness relationship, and provide residence participants continuous assurance and support. For further discussion of courage as an adult education ideal refer to Ohliger (2001, p. 16).

Courage and Henry David Thoreau

> Here is this vast, savage, howling mother of ours, Nature, lying all around, with such beauty, and such affection for her children, as the leopard; and yet we are so early weaned from her breast to society, to that culture which is exclusively an interaction of man on man—a sort of breeding in and in, which produces at most a merely English nobility, a civilization destined to have a speedy limit. (Thoreau, 1862/1977, p. 621)

One voice barely audible when the adult education movement was formed in 1926 was that of Henry David Thoreau, a strong proponent of courage as a life-guiding force. Much of Thoreau's wisdom seems especially pertinent to planners of adult residential education programs in wilderness areas. A strong proponent of individual freedoms, Thoreau embraced simplicity, sensation, sauntering, wildness, youthful curiosity, living in the present, and nature as elixirs of sorts for a deadening of the human spirit often brought about by "civilized" societies. His essay *Walking*, printed posthumously in 1862, seems especially relevant.

Throughout the essay, Thoreau contrasted the cultural achievements of society with the raw embrace of Nature. Residential learning programs held in wilderness settings are uniquely situated to capitalize on the contrast between natural and civilized environments. As noted earlier, a striking component and benefit of residential programs is the conscious removal of individuals from daily societal responsibilities and expectations.

For Thoreau, the "walking" spirit was attitudinal as well as physical. Though he might walk 20 miles without passing a house (a sure sign of civilized life), Thoreau stated that his objective was more to wander about than it was to actually go somewhere specific. For Thoreau, the art of walking was making himself available to novel moments and experiencing the unexpected. In such walks, with heightened senses, the learning he desired from nature was enhanced.

Thoreau equated walking with adventure, not exercise. Fields, woods, and mountains provided Thoreau with the adventures he sought, and though his body physically navigated the route, it was his spirit that guided the adventure. He sought to lose himself completely in these outings, to become totally immersed in the moment, to forget all, and to think about nothing but that which his senses spread before him.

Thoreau weighed the cultural achievements of a society against the concessions individuals made to retain membership in that society. He saw in these concessions a taming of the human spirit. For Thoreau, such concessions led to a dulling of the spirit and a loss of freedom—the freedom to be spontaneous, unpredictable, individual, and truly wild. One way to reclaim a sense of self, which Thoreau saw as the wild self within, was through the physical and mental excursions provided by sauntering, a theme we discuss more fully in Chapter 5.

For Thoreau, knowledge, though useful, was overrated and often led to arrogance and conceit. He believed that ignorance could actually be beautiful if it manifested itself in sincerity and humility, and a genuine openness to new ideas and experiences.

> My desire for knowledge is intermittent; but my desire to bathe my head in atmosphere unknown to my feet is perennial and constant. The highest that we can attain to is not Knowledge, but Sympathy with Intelligence—a novel and grand surprise on a sudden revelation of the insufficiency of all that we call Knowl-

edge before—a discovery that there are more things in heaven and earth than are dreamed of in our philosophy. (1862/1977, p. 623)

Thoreau also cautioned against the folly of dwelling on the past and spending too much time planning for the future—common adult behaviors often reinforced in civilized life. Enjoy the moment, he encouraged, live each day in the present. To read more about the life of Thoreau, refer to Harding, 1992.

RECLAIMING THE INNER CHILD

Thoreau felt the concessions of membership to "civilized society" required a loss of the freedom to be truly wild. Children might act this way, but adults must abide by the "rules" of civilization. As noted earlier, Thoreau embraced simplicity, living in the present, and youthful curiosity as powerful elixirs for a deadening of the human spirit brought about by civilization. These are critical elements to include in residential education experiences for adults. Life in residence is simple in many respects. It allows participants to retreat from or set aside responsibilities and focus on being truly present—more fully connected to the setting and to other participants. Accommodations are basic and the responsibilities of home are left behind. The senses are reawakened and the present becomes paramount through continuous, prolonged activity in a novel environment. Thoreau's prescription for reawakening the spirit reinforces some of the key differences we have observed between the needs of children and adults attending residence programs. Table 1.1 illustrates these differences.

When working with school-aged children, the grades generally considered to be optimal for learning in residence are fourth to sixth (9–12 year olds). At this age children can be quite independent, and they are often eager to test their wings. The cusp of adolescence represents a window of opportunity within which residential education experiences can be a highly effective method for promoting responsibility, bonding with nature, and tolerating others. Because the internal critic has not

Table 1.1 Summary of general difference between children and adults in residence

Children (pre-adolescent)	Adults
Need opportunities to act like adults (to be independent from parents)	Need opportunities to act like children
Respond well to increased responsibility in residence	Respond well to decreased responsibility in residence
Benefit from opportunities for group living/life skills experience	Have less need for group living/life skills experience
Only know how to be themselves (especially true for the very young)	Need to reconnect with essential self (casualty of socialization)
Provide immediate feedback that is easy to read	Provide feedback that is more difficult to read (result of socialization)
Need structure and supervision for reflective/downtime	Need less structure for reflective/downtime; are more likely to self-select safe, appropriate activities
Need less activity level options	Need activity levels to reflect diverse abilities
Are less likely to arrive with their own agendas (preconceived list of expectations)	Are more likely to arrive with their own agendas based on unique histories
Engage easily in creative endeavors	Engage less freely in creative endeavors (creativity needs nurturing)
Live usually in the present	Are less attuned to the present (are more likely to occupy themselves with the past and the future)
Need program content structured in such a way as to build upon previous learning	Need program content structured to recognize that some unlearning may be required

yet emerged, and conformation to a peer group is not yet imperative, this age, from our experience, is generally the peak of flexibility, adaptability, and creativity.

The idea that residential experiences for adults in wilderness areas reawaken the child within comes from our direct ob-

servations, experiences, and the comments of program participants. These childlike qualities include curiosity, being fully present, playfulness, sensation, creativity, and being fully one's self.

The "youthful curiosity," of which Thoreau referred, was
described by Rachel Carson as a "sense of wonder," and it goes
hand in hand with the ability to be fully observant and present.
Carson wrote:

> A child's world is fresh and new and beautiful, full of wonder
> and excitement. It is our misfortune that for most of us that clear-
> eyed vision, that true instinct for what is beautiful and awe-
> inspiring, is dimmed and even lost before we reach adulthood. If
> I had influence with the good fairy who is supposed to preside
> over the christening of all children I should ask that her gift to
> each child in the world be a sense of wonder so indestructible
> that it would last throughout adult life as an antidote against the
> boredom and disenchantments of later years, the sterile preoccu-
> pation with things that are artificial, the alienation from the
> sources of our strength. (1965, pp. 42–43)

Somewhere in the course of daily living, somewhere be-
neath the heavy encrustation of responsibility and routine, the
ability to simply sit, and watch and wonder gradually disap-
pears. Theodore Geisel, better known as Dr. Seuss, referred to
adults as "obsolete children" in the subtitle of his book, *You're
Only Old Once!* (1986).

Adults are all still children at heart, but with each passing
year, they find it increasingly difficult to be fully present—to sa-
vor each moment. Adults spend too much time inside, both inside their own heads, as well as indoors, and as a result they can
feel alienated from others as well as from the earth. As William
Wordsworth expressed in his familiar sonnet penned in 1807,

> The world is too much with us; late and soon,
> Getting and spending, we lay waste our powers:
> Little we see in Nature that is ours. (1932, p. 349)

One can only wonder how Wordsworth would feel about
the human experience in this new century. Yet inside, all are
born for the outside. Adults breathe in and breathe out. Adults

need sun, rain, and soil as surely as the most tentative seedling. Time spent with nature gives back a sense of belonging and connection, as well as a sense of wonder.

Poet Mary Oliver, winner of the Pulitzer Prize for Poetry and the National Book Award, possesses extraordinary perception for wonder in nature—wonder that goes far beyond entertainment or diversion. Mary Oliver reveals our inherent strengths as living, wild creatures. She reminds us of our capacity to adapt, to learn, to thrive. While wilderness may not always be a gentle host, it is always an inspiring teacher. The message is, life is not easy, but the natural world offers infinite opportunities for growth and healing. In the poem "Wild Geese" (1992, p. 110), we are reminded of the sources of our strength and belonging through strong images of migrating geese, mountains, rivers and sweeping rains. We are told that the world calls to us "like wild geese, harsh and exciting—over and over announcing your place in the family of things." Our lives are intimately tied to a much larger and more vital picture than often imagined.

In addition to a capacity for wonder and being fully present, reclaiming the inner child evokes "playfulness." Playfulness was clearly evident one evening we spent with an adult group on the shores of Yellowstone Lake. Having finished dinner at the Lake Hotel after a long day of touring the west side of the park, we were ready for the drive north to our dormitories. Well into the course, all were tired as we boarded the bus. However, the evening was so astonishingly beautiful its last moments demanded savoring, so we made an unscheduled stop along the sandy north shore of Yellowstone Lake. We found ourselves alone as the sun's pink afterglow gave way to a yellow moon rising full over the lake. The clear water sparkled and rippled, breaking in a gentle shush along the obsidian-flecked sand. It was pure magic, and observing was not enough. Despite the cool September temperature, shoes and socks were shed in happy piles, and pants rolled as adults walked, then ran and splashed along the shore. Years were shed in faces illuminated by moonlight and the joy of getting into the game itself—feeling cold wet sand under bare feet. People laughed and shouted and skipped. At no other time during the course did the young child so playfully poke the aging adult in the ribs.

A playful attitude exhibited by instructors may provide a nudge, but the ideal is attained when the behavior is spontaneous. Sometimes facilitators have to know when to get out of the way and simply let such moments unfold. Allowing direct experience with nature and encouraging exploration using all of the senses can help world-weary adults recapture the simple, unsophisticated, and natural joys of childhood.

Perhaps the ability to play is an art to be cultivated. Adults often feel foolish when they play, and they must feel safe from ridicule if it is to occur. Consider these comments from residence program participants (Fleming, 1996):

> I looked around and here were all these adults, down on their hands and knees playing with these bugs. It took all I could do to keep from laughing. And then I thought, Now you look just as silly as the rest of them. (p. 240)
> It was fun. It was pure fun, and there seemed to be no constraints on behavior and thought. (p. 250)
> They did their program, and it was a delightful program, but they got to the point where they finished. And we all just kinda' stood around looking at each other, like, this isn't over yet. And some unidentified motivation—just everybody dancing—and it just really loosened up, and for me, that was significant because— that's when I felt that this is a safe environment. I can be foolish now because everybody else is being foolish and this is what we're doing. (pp. 235–236)

It can take a great deal of courage to make a fool out of yourself in front of others. Yet when people feel safe—part of a supportive learning community—they are not afraid to play and be "foolish." When willing to play and try new things with no real goal other than to have fun, creativity flourishes. Creative work is fun, yet nurturing creativity is no frivolous goal. In the words of another residence participant:

> I think safety and security and I don't know, but it just amazed me, the creativity. And just that I found it in myself that I never knew was there, and I kind of got in touch with that a little bit.

Just the writing, and the chance for some self-reflection. I think that's really important. (Fleming, 1996, p. 244)

Julia Cameron has written at length on reawakening creativity in adults. She refered to the artist self as the "creative child" who must be restored to health:

To restore the artist-child to health we must be willing to go to any lengths—to undertake a pilgrimage, with all the challenges that implies. If this sounds daunting, like an awful lot of work, let me assure you that what we are going to undertake is something radically different from what you might conceive. Because our aim is to strengthen and heal a creative child, we will be undertaking instead a whole lot of play—movement, writing, sight, sound and silence—we will work, yes, but we will really learn to play. (1996, p. 5)

Finally, being childlike means being one's truest self. There is no need to remind a pre-adolescent child, "to thine own self be true." Indeed, it is all they are capable of. Yet it can be a great struggle to those more traveled in years and adversity. The more fully adults understand themselves, in all their complexities, the more confidently and courageously they can move through life's challenges. When adults act from their truest selves, when they follow their hearts, they are most powerful and most capable of fulfilling their great potential to lead productive, joyful lives.

RESIDENTIAL ADULT EDUCATION IN WILDERNESS SETTINGS

Any environmental or experiential outdoor educator will say that teaching about wilderness is best done in wilderness settings. Programs attempting to teach about living organisms and natural processes should occur, if not in a wilderness setting, then at least in a natural setting—be that a nature center, a local park, or a school yard. While there are many definitions of environmental or outdoor education, a most comprehensive one is, "Outdoor education is education 'in', 'about', and 'for' the out-of-doors."

The primary placement of the word "in" is significant. Forest ecology should be taught in a forest, water ecology at a pond or stream, and winter ecology in the snow. While some environmental educators argue the point, most believe there is a place for classroom-based environmental education. A few reasons justifying this position are money, time, and environmental impact. Even within a classroom setting, doing something is preferable to talking about something. Experience is the best teacher. The National Science Education Standards state, "The best way to learn science is by doing science" (1995, p.12). Teach about wilderness in wilderness settings. Of course, this makes sense. Applications of this basic tenet to fields outside environmental education make equal sense, especially in the realm of skill development: a person cannot be taught computer skills without a computer, learn to draw or paint without a pencil or a paintbrush, learn to ski without putting on a pair of skis, or learn to write without putting thoughts on paper. Poet Theodore Roethke said, "I learn by going where I have to go" (1966, p. 108).

To presume that wilderness settings are only appropriate educationally for teaching wilderness topics is selling wilderness far short. The unique attributes of wilderness settings for educational purposes have been long recognized and are widely implemented—summer camps, juvenile justice programs, leadership schools, and retreats of all sorts. It is not coincidental that the main goals of these programs overlap with those most frequently associated with residential experiences for adults: building relationships and personal change. Wilderness programs are also typically residential in nature, spanning weeks or months. The added component of wilderness can both facilitate and extend into new realms the gains typically associated with residencies.

Adult Residential Education

Adult education researcher Jean Anderson Fleming has studied residential learning and drawn some useful conclusions (1998). She identified three descriptive themes: relationship building, learning, and individual change. Relationships develop differently, more quickly and more intensely, in residential settings because associations are different from those found in a normal classroom. When people live, learn, work, and play together, there is a heightened sense of fellowship, togetherness, community, and family. Learning is enhanced because students are immersed in their subject. The learning is contextual and free time is often spent in discussion of subject matter. People say they change both during and following residential experiences. They report that they feel safe while in a residential setting. They feel they can let go, loosen up, and be foolish. They begin to write, draw, and be creative. They feel an increase in their sense of self-worth and in their tolerance and understanding of others.

Fleming (1998) also identified two overarching themes that, when woven throughout a residential program, help make relationship building, learning, and change possible. These are detachment and continuity. Detachment refers to the physical and psychological isolation that occurs either because of the remote location or by program design. The world of the participant is restricted to the program, and the choice of companions is limited. Continuity refers to the continuous, uninterrupted nature of the experience. Participants live together 24 hours a day for days or weeks. During this time, they are uninterrupted by outside distractions and pressures. This allows time to focus on the subject as well as time for self-reflection.

Not to minimize the relationship building, learning, and change taking place outside of residential settings, Bersch and Fleming acknowledged, "We experience these phenomena all the time in our daily lives as well as in nonresidential programs. Residential education, however, seems to promote more rapid, yet more intense and more profound, changes than are probable with other formats" (1997, p. 52). They also suggested, that while any residential program format can promote these outcomes, perhaps the best (fastest, most effective) was the residential program in a wilderness setting. Furthermore, in addition to enhancing relationship building, wilderness settings push personal change and self-awareness in some unique and predictable directions, enhancing the childlike qualities of playfulness, creativity, and curiosity.

As mentioned previously, the physical and psychological detachment possible with residential learning creates vast potential for individual growth and change. While simply being out of a normal routine with all of its distracting pressures can foster this sense of detachment, a natural setting can add benefits beyond those possible at a large hotel in an urban location. As noted by Bersch and Fleming,

> [A natural setting] is aesthetically appealing, where the pace of life is slower and the distracting temptations of cities are avoided. It is also important that participants be able to enjoy simple pleasures, taking walks outside to break up their days—[which] will help foster a renewed feeling of cohesion and will allow participants to be much more reflective, creative, focused and productive (1997, p. 53).

Bersch and Fleming also suggested that remote natural settings could promote a sense of "adventure and authentic experience" (p. 53). They went on to state,

> [Wilderness areas could also provide] a multisensory experience that seems to heighten learning and magnify feelings. Just being in a different setting may provide a disorienting dilemma for participants, which may be the first step in a process of personal or perspective transformation. . . . Perhaps there is indeed a healing power in nature that can be used to help learners relax and grow into their potential (1997, p. 54).

Bersch and Fleming go on to note that nature may actually provide an environment for relaxation, growth and healing.

The Healing Power of Nature

The natural world and other organisms have been shown to exert positive influences on health, especially if health is defined somewhat broadly as the World Health Organization did in 1948, "as a state of complete physical, mental and social well-being and not merely the absence of disease and infirmity." Consider these cases in point excerpted from Wilson (2002):

- Studies of patient response prior to surgery and dental work have consistently revealed a significant reduction of stress in the presence of plants and aquaria. Natural environments viewed through windows or merely displayed in wall-mounted pictures produce the same effect.
- Postsurgical patients recover more quickly, suffer fewer minor complications, and need smaller dosages of painkillers if given a window view of open terrain or waterscape.
- In one Swedish study covering 15 years of records, clinically anxious psychiatric patients responded positively to wall pictures of natural environments, but negatively, occasionally even violently, to most other decorations (especially those containing abstract art).
- Comparable studies in prisons revealed that inmates provided window views of nearby farmlands and forests, as opposed to prison yards, reported fewer stress-related symptoms such as headaches and indigestion.
- In a different category, the popular notion that owning pets reduces stress-related problems has been well supported by research conducted independently in Australia, England, and the United States. In one Australian study, which factored out variation in exercise levels, diet, and social class, pet ownership accounted for a statistically significant reduction of cholesterol, triglycerides, and systolic blood pressure. In a parallel U.S. study, survivors of heart attacks (myocardial infarction) who owned dogs had a survival rate six times higher than those who did not.

Why individuals respond positively to natural environments and other life forms is an intriguing question. Wilson (1984) classified this propensity as a true human instinct—something immutable that individuals are born with, not taught. Human beings are bound to the environment by "a sense of genetic unity, kinship and deep history" (Wilson, 2002, p. 133).

People, it seems, not only harbor an innate affinity for natural environments, but exhibit a clear preference for savanna, or park-like habitat. The ideal human habitat seems to include a long depth of view, a smooth ground surface dotted with trees, and location near a body of water. A genetic basis for such a preference is suggested by its manifestation across cultures, and supports the "savanna hypothesis"—that humanity originated in the savannas and transitional forests of Africa, and spent the vast majority of its evolutionary history in this ancestral habitat (Wilson, 1984, p. 136). We feel good in certain environments because they stimulate pleasurable sensations in brains that are inherently adapted to such habitat.

SUMMARY

In this chapter, we provided numerous rationales for conducting residential adult education programs in wilderness areas. We made a case for why strengthening the bonds between adults and wild things (found within as well as outside) is worthwhile for individuals as well as for wilderness areas. We suggested that the strengthening of these bonds often requires courage—the courage to become reacquainted with the inner child, the courage to reconnect to wild places, and the courage to live in the present. Residential programs are ideal environments for playfulness and unleashing creativity. When conducted in wilderness areas, such environments are also conducive for intensifying relationships and clarifying understandings.

The next three chapters explore the nuts and bolts of planning, conducting, and concluding residential adult education in wilderness areas. Chapters 5 and 6 offer some specific strategies for experiencing and reflecting upon time spent in wilderness areas.

CHAPTER 2

Planning an Event

Planning a residential program is similar to planning any large event. Mostly, it requires good organizational skills and attention to detail. Much of what follows may sound like common sense. Yet it can be hugely comforting to be able to sit down with someone who has been through this process many times and has, over time, adjusted the planning to fit the unique needs of residential programs for adults in wilderness settings. The purpose of this section is to provide such a conversation. We hope these chapters supply the necessary nuts and bolts to allow the residence planner to proceed with confidence in knowing that essentials are not overlooked. The outcome should be an efficient and comprehensive plan for the best possible program. We identify the major tasks in the checklist in Figure 2.1.

FORM A PLANNING COMMITTEE

Planning a residential program is a huge job. It should not be taken on by one person. That said, it is essential that someone provide leadership. A planning committee should include individuals knowledgeable and capable of performing the following major functions: leadership, administration, program design, and marketing. If meals will be provided by caterers, include the caterers in your planning committee as well. Make sure committee members have clearly defined roles and understand expectations for their participation. Committee membership and responsibilities might break out as follows.

Pre-Program Task Checklist

___ Form a planning committee.
___ Create a shared program vision.
___ Generate and investigate program ideas.
___ Make a selection.
___ Develop themes, goals, and objectives.
___ Strive for a combination of experiences.
___ Determine schedule and staffing needs.
___ Find a location and a facility.
___ Plan to take people outdoors and get moving.
___ Determine best method for provision of meals.
___ Prepare a budget and determine fees.
___ Market the program.
___ Send an informational packet to registered participants.

Figure 2.1 The Pre-program Task Checklist

Committee Chair

This person's primary function is to provide leadership for the committee. The chair selects the committee, calls the meetings, communicates and guides the vision, helps set goals, establishes deadlines, and provides feedback.

Administration

This person is responsible for budget tracking, fee collection, dispersal of funds, instructor and caterer contracts, facility rental, permits, fee waivers, vehicle rental, and equipment allocation.

Program Coordinator/Lead Instructor

This person is the primary program designer, working out the details of what the program will look like. Responsibilities include selecting topic and theme, writing an agenda, teaching all or part of the program, making speaker arrangements, facilitating guest speakers, and communicating with registered participants. In addition, this person usually provides the text for the flier or brochure announcing the program and takes the lead in assembling the pre-course packet. Other responsibilities might include fielding phone calls and emails pertaining to specific questions and concerns about the program, and providing material for marketing needs.

Marketing

This person is responsible for advertising and publicity and should understand the marketing environment of the service area. Advertising refers specifically to paid forms of promotion, such as newspaper, radio, and direct mailing. Publicity usually refers to unpaid promotion. Publicity might include partnering with other organizations to get the word out, writing a press release, posting fliers, starting a listserv, or presenting at conferences or fairs. The marketing environment is assessed through demographics, economic climate, environmental issues, political climate, and cultural considerations. This knowledge can help predict how people find out about things in the community. Adults with a high level of education tend to look to media and experts as sources of information, while adults with less formal education tend to rely mainly on conversations with family and friends (Knox, 1981). If there are already many similar programs being offered in the area, consider collaboration.

Catering

This person is responsible for providing meals during the course. Caterers must be capable of meeting the unique needs of the facility and setting, as well as individual dietary needs. Wilderness settings can present unique challenges to caterers, such as lengthy transportation to the site, regulations prohibiting the use of outdoor fires for grilling, or special food storage regulations. Adult education groups often include individuals on special diets. Furthermore, residential programs typically are subject to ongoing schedule adjustments—a late return from a long hike due to weather, an unplanned opportunity for wildlife viewing, or a vehicle breakdown. It is essential that caterers be flexible people, and desirable that they understand the program and feel a part of the group. Invite them to attend as many planning meetings as possible, as well as to attend as many program sessions as possible during the event.

Begin planning a year in advance and check in with committee members on a regularly scheduled basis—weekly typically works well. This will keep the momentum going and preclude the need for overly long meetings. The remainder of this chapter details the major planning committee tasks in roughly chronological order.

CREATE A SHARED PROGRAM VISION

A specific program may or may not already be imagined when the planning process begins. Even if a rough idea exists, it is a good idea to work with a committee to create a shared vision for the program. Take the time to discuss and develop core values or guiding beliefs. What follows is a list of our guiding beliefs with regard to residential experiences in wilderness settings:

We believe that—

- Adults should have the opportunity to attend a residential education experience at some point in their lives.
- Adult education professionals should have the opportunity to provide such an experience, thereby enriching their own education.
- Experience is the best teacher and past experience is the primary building block for learning.
- Learning programs should be conducted holistically: attending to intellectual, emotional, and physical domains.

- For maximal learning and growth, participants need to feel safe: physically, from the personal judgment of others, and from academic judgment and pressures.
- Residential programs in wilderness settings are great equalizers. All participants must meet the same fundamental challenges. Professors, administrators, students, CEOs, employees—all become colleagues when stripped of titles and suits.
- Residential settings, free from pressures, roles, responsibilities, and routines of daily life, allow continuous, uninterrupted, structured, and unstructured learning possibilities.
- Mysterious, unpredictable, and exciting things happen in wilderness settings.
- Wilderness settings offer outstanding opportunities for contemplation and developing relationships.
- Relationships develop quickly and intensely in residential settings.
- The positive results of relationship building enhance the educational experience and can build a strong and enduring sense of community.
- Residential experiences in wilderness settings can access playful, creative expression in adults and a sense of renewal or re-connection with the "inner child" or "essential self."
- A residential experience in a wilderness setting often results in individual change and personal growth.
- Natural environments are underutilized educationally.
- Natural environments exert a positive influence on health—mental and physical; at least 50% of course time should be spent outside.
- People are better equipped to make informed resource decisions if they have a strong base-line education in natural resources.
- Residential education experiences in wilderness settings promote appreciation and responsibility for preserving wilderness.
- A global land ethic must be fostered to ensure the health of the planet.

A discussion of guiding beliefs can go a long way toward creating a shared vision. Topic is important, but guiding beliefs are equally important considerations for program planning. Begin with guiding beliefs, then progress to topic selection.

GENERATE AND INVESTIGATE PROGRAM IDEAS

Members of the planning committee feel a sense of achievement once they can identify and agree upon a program theme, so work on topics, title, and agenda early on. This will allow the marketing person to get going, and marketing does need to occur concurrently with planning. The fact that planning committee members are "riding the bicycle while they are building it" is typical and should not be overly distressing!

To arrive at a program topic, try asking these questions: What kinds of things are people in the community interested in? Who is the audience? (If a broader audience is desirable, seek them out and welcome them in.) What topics does the environment suggest? How might current environmentally based political issues spark interest in educational topics? What expertise exists locally and who might wish to contribute to the program? Addressing these questions can help guide program selection. Also, review past program evaluations, especially if feedback was solicited on what kinds of programs participants would like to see offered in the future. Interview or conduct focus groups with participants as well as non-participants for new ideas. Review comparable programs being offered by others.

MAKE A SELECTION

In selecting the best option from a variety of possibilities, ask the following questions: Does this program advance the mission of the institution? Does it complement other offerings? Does it have the potential to improve the quality of adult lives? Does it involve collaboration with other organizations while maintaining the institution's identity? Does it fit available resources (personnel, facilities, money, and equipment)?

DEVELOP THEMES, GOALS, AND OBJECTIVES

Select a program theme that creatively encompasses all the pieces the planning committee would like to include. Focus may be broad or narrow, but keep in mind that the topic may be new to most if not all program participants. Do not assume prior topic knowledge with adult education groups. Successful programs of ours based in Yellowstone have included "Heart of a Continent"—a broad treatment of Yellowstone's wildlife, geology, and cultural history; "Where the Wild Things Are: Autumn on Yellowstone's Northern Range"—a more narrow focus on five primary wildlife species; and "Lamar Landscapes: Focusing on Our Wild Nature"—experiencing the park as an inspirational setting for writing and photography.

Goals and objectives should be clearly written, communicated, and understood by instructors and participants. Clear objectives guide content, methods, and evaluation. Articulating objectives ensures that program descriptions in brochures, catalogs, and websites are accurate and informative. This will also allow participants to match their own objectives with the appropriate residence program.

STRIVE FOR A COMBINATION OF EXPERIENCES

A single-faceted program is like a plain cheese pizza. Plain may satisfy some appetites, but most adult learners appreciate a little more complexity of flavor. From our experience, the most appealing programs for adults seem to be "combos." Or, as business consultant Joseph Pine has said, they are "all-encompassing, with entertaining, educational, escapist, or aesthetic elements" (1999, p. 3). Providing a diversity of experiences often speaks to a diversity of interests.

Based upon their work in adult education, Sachatello-Sawyer, Fellenz, Burton, Gittings-Carlson, Lewis-Mahony, and Woolbaugh provided a list of types of experiences excellent adult museum programs generally provide; this list seems equally applicable to designing residence experiences in wilderness areas (2002, p. 145):

- Knowledge acquisition (grasping new ideas, actively learning something new)
- Practical skill building (trying something new, learning a new skill)
- Physical challenges (physical activities or sports)
- Interpersonal interactions (sharing personal stories, discovering relationships)
- Spiritual connections (connections with life, death, spirits, the paranormal)
- Aesthetic experience (immersion in art, music, or landscape)
- Outdoor adventure (immersion in a new or disorienting environment)
- Entertainment (fun activities, humorous instructor or participants)

DETERMINE SCHEDULE AND STAFFING NEEDS

The time of year a residence program is offered may be limited by availability and accessibility of facilities as well as by the availability of key instructors. The time of year may also influence who can attend the program. For example, teachers and graduate students may be more likely to attend a summer course than one scheduled during the school year. Retired people may make up the majority of a class offered in September. Generally, people prefer not to drive long distances when roads may be icy or snowy.

Recruit the best possible staff for desired sessions. Observe possible instructors, follow up on recommendations from others, and keep in mind the qualities that make a good instructor. Seek instructors with experience and credibility. Look for presenters who have taught adults before, who encourage participation, are sensitive to the needs of seniors, and are dynamic and engaging. Instructors should be able to communicate with a diversity of people, and be able to present ideas in a way that is comprehensible to a broad audience. Also, they should be good listeners. They should be professional and flexible. Vibrant personalities and accessible demeanors put participants at ease and often infect them with enthusiasm for the subject. Instructors should demonstrate a real love for teaching—a sense that they want to be there and gain as much as they give. The best instructors seem to be people who have passion, creativity, and the ability to make connections between diverse topics. Perhaps most important is the relationship between the teacher and the learner. Freeman Tilden was widely revered as a teacher, mentor and philosopher; in his later years he worked extensively with the National Park Service and produced his seminal work, *Interpreting Our Heritage* (1957/1977). In this book, Tilden stated that despite the promise of "new" telecommunication "gadgetry," there will never be a substitute "as satisfactory as the direct contact not merely with the voice, but with the hand, the eye, the casual and meaningful ad lib, and with that something which flows out of the very constitution of the individual in his physical self" (p. 95).

Wilderness settings demand additional skills, especially of instructors expected to present field sessions. Wilderness trip leaders need to be knowledgeable and experienced with regard to safe conduct in wilderness settings. They should minimally be trained in Wilderness First Aid. For more information on this 16-hour certification course, contact the National Outdoor Leadership School (NOLS) Wilderness Medicine Institute (n.d.) at its website. Instructors need to be well versed in the nuances of best practices for teaching out of doors. These include how to minimize distractions, how to take advantage of the environment the group is in, how to move groups while maintaining engagement, where and how often to make stops and where to best position themselves to be heard, how to monitor comfort and a myriad of other details that all add up to the difference between a highly enjoyable and enlightening field experience and one that amounts to little more than a lecture without the benefit of chairs and a sound system. Perhaps most important, outdoor educators must be flexible. When most effective, they are constantly adjusting their activity to the environment and the group.

Though many of our instructors conduct programs as a routine aspect of their positions (for example natural resource agency personnel), some require payment. In these cases a formal contract should be developed, defining responsibilities and payment.

FIND A LOCATION AND A FACILITY

"Wilderness" for our purposes, is a loose, somewhat subjective moniker. It can encompass a wide range of possible program locations, which might include parks (national, state, and city), forests, refuges, or private property. What is most important is that the location and program topic be redundant. As the National Park Service suggests, "teach the real thing in the right place." The distinction is context—unlike teaching using museum objects, or fish in an aquarium (real things, but out of context), wild and historic settings add the opportunity to gain a more complex, informative, holistic understanding of the topic. There is something engaging and immediate when a person hears, "it happened right here," or "it is happening right now." Place is powerful. If the topic is geology, program location should be an interesting and accessible place to "see" geology. If planning a program on desert ecology, do not schedule it in a wetland, no matter how perfect the wetland-based facility may be. While this may seem rather obvious, the converse is also true and further illuminates the importance of place.

Ellen once attended a weeklong training class in Yellowstone that had absolutely nothing to do with the park. The course involved a pairing of informal (park) educators from across the country with formal (K-12) educators from matching locations. The primary purpose was to train participants in the implementation of national curriculum standards, specifically towards the goal of enriching science education by facilitating learning in parks. It was a useful and ambitious project, and the schedule was filled with a diversity of stakeholders from universities, agencies, and professional associations—all flown to this remote location at considerable expense. Unfortunately, many of the attendees erroneously assumed they would have the opportunity to experience Yellowstone—perhaps not all 2.2 million acres, but at least some of its most famous attractions. This was not to be. The collective frustration became noticeable as hour after hour, day after day people sat in a conference room while perfect fall days slipped away and rutting elk bugled and sparred within earshot. Given the goals and content of the training, it would have been more effectively conducted in an easily accessible urban location without the "distractions" of the park. What is best suited to the classroom, teach in the classroom. What is best suited to wilderness, teach in wilderness.

Beyond the practical pairing of location with topic, also consider the basic desirability of isolation for fostering a sense of detachment from everyday life. This sense of feeling apart and isolated from the everyday world and all its distractions is essential to maximize the benefits of residential learning. But how far away does one have to go to get away from it all? And which "conveniences" must one give up to screen out the static of daily life and tune in to the environment and the present? Is no TV good enough, or should participants also be deprived of radio, newspaper, and hair dryer? The best mix of deprivation and comfort depends upon your program goals. Generally speaking, "rustic" is good. In their study of residential programs, Bersch and Fleming (1997) observed,

> In places that lack the usual routine amenities people shift from being concerned with material comforts to focusing on their physical surroundings or the spiritual dimensions of their experience: there may be no running water or electricity, but there is good food, great scenery, and great beauty (p. 54).

Do keep in mind as a program planner, however, that "too rustic" may in practice translate into considerable time devoted to basic functions, like staying warm, dry, hydrated, and fed. Unless the topic of the program is wilderness camping, it is probably preferable to secure a facility with potable water, a fully equipped kitchen, dining room, bathrooms, showers, and beds.

Finally, the wilderness facility should ideally model environmentally sustainable practices including energy efficiency, water conservation, recycling, and other waste reduction practices.

PLAN TO TAKE PEOPLE OUTDOORS
AND GET MOVING

Being physically active is healthful for the mind as well as the body and should be actively promoted during residential wilderness programs. While the physical benefits of exercise have long been acknowledged, the relationship between physical activity and brain function is a more recent discovery, and is especially applicable for older adults. It seems that physical fitness and mental fitness do go together. Faculty of the Harvard Medical School (2004) have stated that regular exercise may help preserve brain function either through improved blood flow to the brain or through the promotion of lung function—better lung function makes more oxygen available to brain cells. Further, animal research shows that exercise increases the levels of substances that encourage brain cell growth and protect them from damage (neurotrophins).

The Harvard Medical School group also pointed out that despite the benefits, 60 percent of Americans engage in too little activity or none at all. One in three women and one in four men ages 65–74 do not pursue any physical leisure activities. Among people age 75 and older, less than one in five report exercising regularly. Part of the problem, of course, is that exercise is no fun for many people. The social setting of a residential course can turn exercise into a fun group activity. For those who suffer painful or disabling disorders, any exercise can be a difficult challenge. With regard to disabilities, limitations should be addressed in advance on a case by case basis, making accommodations where possible. As noted in the previous chapter, research indicates that simply being outdoors in a natural environment, even without the added benefits of exercise, is healthful for the mind and the body.

Physical exercise in the outdoors can occur both formally through scheduled sessions as well as informally via individual initiative in the early mornings or evenings. Expect a wide range of capabilities as well as a diversity of expectations with regard to the physical requirements of the course. Often the best strategy is detailed communication prior to the course and the provision of choices during the program. Provide encouragement as well as suggested activities and necessary safety information relative to the area for those desiring to strike out on their own.

To set expectations for physical activity include in the agenda the altitude at which activities will occur, the distance to be covered in any field sessions involving hiking, the elevation gain, the terrain, the pace, as well as the purpose of the hike and what participants are likely to see. The more detailed the description, the better. If bathrooms are not available on longer hikes, people should know about this. How bathroom stops will be handled should be discussed before the group is out on the trail. Much useful information with regard to minimum impact practices in wilderness areas is available. One excellent source is the interagency sponsored "Leave No Trace" outdoor ethics program (n.d.).

In addition to providing detailed information concerning physical activity in advance of the program, encourage potential and registered participants to contact the lead instructor with any concerns or questions.

Encourage participants to start walking prior to arrival at the residence. If the program will be held at altitude, remind those coming from lower elevations that their aerobic capacity will be diminished at first, resulting in shortness of breath. Heart patients especially may have difficulties at altitude. It takes the body approximately two weeks to fully acclimate to the decreased oxygen levels at altitude (there is a physiological adjustment of oxygen release by hemoglobin in the bloodstream). Assure those from sea level that keeping hydrated and engaging in aerobic activity actually speeds the acclimatization process.

We have found it very helpful when working with adults to offer two activity level options for hikes: "less active" and "more active." The more active option might require four miles of travel and some climbing. The less active choice would typically be under a mile, occur at a slower pace, on level terrain.

Each day both options are offered with participants self-selecting the outing they feel most comfortable doing. Ideally both options should be lead, with similar content goals achieved during each. Once the entire group is back together, allow time to compare and share experiences.

The above pre-event planning steps should minimize last minute surprises and adjustments due to fitness levels, but adjustments may still need to be made once participants arrive and as needs develop during the program. Remember, all participants need to feel safe both physically and from the judgment of others for maximal program benefit.

DETERMINE BEST METHOD FOR PROVISION OF MEALS

Meals can be handled through individual responsibility, shared responsibility (with or without hired cooks), or fully catered. Some residence programs adopt a combination of a few or all of these options. There are advantages and disadvantages to each approach.

With individual responsibility, participants bring and prepare meals for themselves. Advantages to this method include lower course fees, fewer organizational tasks, and individual responsibility for dietary restrictions. Individuals may also find they enjoy sharing kitchen tasks and informally share prepared dishes—food preparation can provide yet another bonding opportunity. One disadvantage is the time it takes large groups to cook and clean, which can be considerable depending upon the individuals and the kitchen setup. If this method is chosen, suggest that participants keep meals simple (providing specific menu suggestions is helpful), and inform them of any food storage limitations, as well as what the facility does and does not provide for their use.

Shared responsibility can mean a number of different things. It might mean that participants bring food, are responsible for their own breakfasts and lunches, but are expected to prepare a dish for all to share for dinner (potluck). It might al-

ternately mean that a leader plans the menu and provides ingredients, but all participants assist with preparation and cleanup
for each meal, usually on a scheduled basis by assigned work
group, with all tasks equally divided over the length of the residence. This route provides a middle ground between the laissez-
faire approach described above and full catering.

Catering is the most expensive route, but has some clear advantages. Meals can be exceptional, adding to the enjoyment of
the experience for many adults. A fully catered residential experience can provide adults with one more measure of relaxation—
a break from the cooking and cleaning they regularly do at
home. It is the most time-efficient method for feeding a large
group, allowing for more program time.

Whichever method chosen, food preparation, serving, and
cleanup should model environmentally sustainable practices to
the greatest extent possible. Discourage excessive use of dispos-
ables, and encourage recycling and other energy efficient and
environmentally sensitive practices in the kitchen.

PREPARE A BUDGET AND DETERMINE FEES

Evaluate expenses and financing. Expenses include costs
for program development, delivery, and evaluation. Key budget
elements to consider include staff and instructor salaries and benefits, advertising and promotional materials, instructional sup-
plies and materials, equipment, facility rental, food, travel, entrance fees, and transportation during the course.

Some residence programs are expected to break even, some
are subsidized, and some are expected to make a profit. Know
which administrative expectation applies to the program, and
plan accordingly.

When analyzing financing, consider the possibility of having
some of the necessary items donated. Possible sources of income
include operating funds from the parent institution; participant
fees; sales from materials, publications, or services; grants; and
profits from past programs. Keep in mind that pricing decisions
affect who can attend and influence interest in and perception

of the program. Consider offering a deferred payment plan, differential pricing, discounting, or scholarships to attract individuals who may not otherwise attend.

When conducting a program in a national park, national forest, national historic site, or any other federal fee collection area, the group may qualify for an entrance fee waiver. Contact the visitor services office at the site and ask them if the group qualifies. If the primary purposes of the program are educational as opposed to recreational it is likely to qualify; generally, the coordinator will be asked to complete an application form.

MARKET THE PROGRAM

Marketing strategies are what gets the word out and ultimately fills the residence program. There are many creative ways to market a program, including a few relating to fees. Special discounts can be offered for repeat program participants, volunteers, early registrants, those who recruit friends, or multiple registrants from the same organization.

The best strategies are determined through an understanding of the marketing climate, a concept discussed at the beginning of this chapter. Some widely applicable suggestions follow.

A program begins the minute a planning committee announces it. Take time in print and electronic media to create the right flavor by providing engaging, detailed descriptions and graphics. When using text, attempt to catch the reader's attention in the first few seconds through logos, photographs, and language. Whet learner appetites by allowing potential participants to "take the trip" while reading the program description. Post direct mailings at least six to ten months in advance so participants can fit the program into their schedules. A sample of an initial program description is included in Appendix A. Always avoid direct mailings around holidays.

Collaboration can help stretch dollars. Many organizations manage large mailing lists and might be willing to add information to a publication or web site free of charge. Potential publicity partners may include chambers of commerce, service clubs

(Rotary, Kiwanis), professional organizations (such as those serving teachers or physicians), public institutions (libraries, universities), businesses (banks, department stores, restaurants), and clubs (gardeners, history buffs) (Satchatello-Sawyer et al., 2002).

For ongoing programs, establish relationships with key media figures (freelance and staff writers, radio announcers) and communicate with them about programming regularly. Invite media figures to attend programs free of charge.

A lot can be learned through tracking hits and misses. Include in the final evaluation a question asking participants how they heard about the program. Having quantitative data helps adjust marketing strategies for the next residential program.

SEND AN INFORMATIONAL PACKET TO REGISTERED PARTICIPANTS

At least two months prior to the residence mail an informational packet to all registered participants. This should include a welcome letter from the instructor(s), the course agenda, maps (showing major routes to the facility, as well as a more detailed map of the facility and surroundings), a clothing and equipment list, suggested readings, and a list of registered participants. See Appendix B for some samples. Providing a list of participants allows people to begin to get to know the group—where they are from and what their names are. Do not provide contact information in advance. If individuals choose to share this information it can be distributed with permission at the close of the program with the disclaimer that this list should not be shared, sold, or used for any purposes other than staying in touch should participants so desire.

SUMMARY

As noted at the beginning of the chapter, planning a residential program is a major undertaking. From our experience, it is fundamental that a team (planning committee) mentality be formed where all members help create and then share a common vision for the program. Successful residential programs involve many tasks and require attention to lots of details, but the results are extremely rewarding. Hopefully, residence coordinators reading this chapter found a road map of sorts to guide their initial planning. The next chapter discusses what we do when the program actually begins.

CHAPTER 3

Conducting an Event

Though it may seem comforting to assume the planning phase is completed once individuals arrive, actually residential programs are rather organic and tweaking and adjustments are continuous. With the arrival of each new participant, the program evolves in unique ways. Still, numerous good practice principles help corral the personal baggage and personal agendas of participants and eventually help form a learning community. There are many things to keep in mind when the program finally begins. The purpose of this chapter is to share some major items: getting started; community building; a typical day; working with program instructors (the slide presentation and the nature field trip); and the wrap-up session. Special attention is given to shaping effective and meaningful learning communities and making the study of the natural world comprehensible.

GETTING STARTED

The first few hours can make or break a residential program. Participants arrive with numerous questions and concerns—many only tangentially related to the program's focus. There are concerns about residential life such as expectations, roommates, choice, responsibilities, and freedoms. There are concerns about facility such as warmth, space, sleeping and dining arrangements, location of rest rooms, and comfort. There are concerns about other participants, such as general compatibility, openness, acceptance, temperaments, and degrees of pleasantness. There are concerns about planning committee members, such as sensitivity, flexibility, interests, overall demeanor, expertise, and organizational skills. And, there are concerns about program content, such as thoroughness, presentation format, familiarity, and preparation. During the first few hours, program planners need to anticipate, acknowledge, and address most, if not all, of these common participant concerns. Management tasks occurring in the first few hours of a program are organized here as greeting participants, the introduction session, and breaking the ice.

Greeting Participants

As noted earlier, initial promotional materials and direct correspondence with the lead instructor should have already set a certain tone for the residence—hopefully one of acceptance and enthusiasm. Now, as participants arrive, some positive verification of the welcoming and supportive environment strived for in earlier descriptions of the program should take place. This verification begins out front of the facility. Members of the planning committee now assume new roles such as initial greeter, registrar, and guides. This is also another good time to anticipate the unexpected; given that so few adults have much recent experience in residential programs, expect the concerns noted above, as well as others, and remain reassuring. Stay relaxed. Though numerous last minute setbacks may occur, such as a broken stove, a running faucet or toilet, the late arrival of caterers, to name but a few, it is imperative program planners take it all in stride and remain upbeat.

Out front in the driveway, the chair of the program committee or one of the lead instructors should personally welcome participants to the facility and to the program. The residence programs discussed in this book are not conferences and it is not enough to place a banner on the grounds directing participants to a sign-in table. Unlike a conference setting where hundreds of guests may arrive at some appointed hour, residence programs often include fewer than 35 people and are therefore rather intimate. A personal touch is required. Greet and welcome all guests. Walk participants into the part of the facility where registration packets are located and introduce them to other members of the planning committee.

Someone in charge of basic registration procedures should next meet program participants. This person provides participants with an updated agenda and packet. Packet materials include maps of the area and facility, a current listing of participants, welcome letter from the Planning Committee, room assignments, program changes or modifications to starting times, and a name card, ideally attached to a cord that can be worn around the neck. This individual should be another enthusiastic contact for participants, completely familiar with the program and able to address most questions. Depending upon the number of participants, it may be necessary for two people to do these tasks. Our preference is to allow check-in to occur over a two-hour time span. This permits flexibility in arrival time and spreads out the work.

Once participants complete the final registration process and receive their packets, provide a brief tour of the grounds and facility, including meeting rooms, kitchen and dining rooms, and sleeping accommodations. During the tour, introduce participants to other guests as well as to general expectations. If participants need to learn about the proper use of stoves, fixtures, or appliances, or if there are food, clothing, or valuables storage issues, cover them at this time. Participants should feel their welfare, comfort, and safety are being addressed and that they are truly welcomed to the residence. Because each guide may spend ten minutes or more with either individual or small groups of participants, it is a good idea to have many members of the planning committee serve this role.

Again, if participants feel program organizers are struggling or hurried, this will often affect their attitude as well. Anticipate the worst, prepare for it as best as possible, and then adjust. If planning committee members behave calmly, so generally will participants. Until some behavior on the part of a program committee member betrays their faith, residence participants generally trust the abilities of organizers to work things out and to deliver a quality learning experience—why else would they register for the program? This seems especially so when it comes to sleeping arrangements.

Sleeping accommodations and rest rooms often are major concerns for participants somewhat used to personal privacies and personal space. It is not uncommon that "reasonably priced" residential accommodations in wilderness areas—in the $25-$35.00 a night range—are rather simple, fairly rustic, and involve sharing both toilets (bath houses) and sleeping quarters. We have used both cabins and dormitories and in every instance the use of common toilets and the sharing of rooms were expected. Though often a "tad" apprehensive, participants generally expect these housing situations to exist and adjust, especially if the residence brochure fully addressed lodging arrangements. Try not to overcrowd rooms. To ease tension somewhat, as participants visit their rooms for the first time, consider placing welcome cards and mints on beds—not a big deal, but it does produce smiles. Wherever possible, allow individuals to identify roommates in advance and plan arrangements with some forethought to the gender and age of participants.

The Introduction Session

We generally prefer to begin a residence in the early evening, allowing participants to travel to the facility and have dinner. Check-in is normally between 5:00—7:00 PM, followed by a brief introduction to the course and, if time allows, an evening session preferably conducted outdoors.

The introduction session should stress three things: expectations, acceptance, and introductions. First, share with participants expectations for the residence and describe the various ways the program is designed to meet expectations. Next, reinforce what should already be emerging as a climate of acceptance in regards to participants and enthusiasm for the residence experience. Finally, learn more about the participants, their backgrounds, and their personal goals for the residence.

In describing expectations, it is useful to address some basic differences between conference and residential programs.

Conference attendees and residence participants expect an introduction session to cover the topics, speakers, sessions, events, and activities that compose the overall focus of the event. But, given that many conferences allow for a fairly significant amount of personal choice in regards to sleeping and meal arrangements, and attendance at sessions often is optional, it is imperative residence participants realize they are in a more structured environment. Therefore it is extremely important to confront this issue and link the perceived benefits of residence to the general goals of the program. These include the general outcomes of residential programs mentioned earlier, such as the intensity of the learning experience, the letting go of many responsibilities, and the working through of new freedoms such as reconnecting to the inner child. It is also important to address the issue of wilderness. Why is the residence being held in a wilderness area? What does wilderness have to do with the topics covered in the program as well as with the personal growth and well being of participants?

In introducing the program itself, try not to present it piecemeal. Surprise is one thing; confusion is another. Provide a complete program overview: general expectations, scheduled presentations and activities, and those times still malleable to the general interests of the groups, as well as general logistics, including arrangements for meals and lodging. Enthusiasm for the program should be apparent to all participants. It is also imperative there is time for questions, exchange, and review. Again, provide the overview in a relaxed manner. Given all the initial preparations and logistics of greeting participants, assigning rooms, providing meals, there is a good possibility the program may already be behind schedule but avoid establishing a "catching-up" tempo by seeming hurried.

Next, continue crafting a supportive learning environment that promotes and attempts to maintain balance of focus throughout the residence—focusing as much upon the participants and their learning as upon subjects and planned activities. This begins with the layout of furniture in the meeting room. To the degree possible, arrange tables and chairs in as close to a circular design as possible so individuals face each other as well as the program planners and presenters. This is a constant and visible reminder that participants are as much the focus of the residence as are the themes addressed. Next, place some water and simple refreshments on the tables and include folded 5x7 cards for participant names. Also check for individual understandings by frequently referring to participants by name.

Finally, it is time for participants and members of the planning committee to introduce themselves. This is a key component of the introduction session and should be conducted thoughtfully. To begin, present a few guiding questions and ask each member of the group to write a brief response. Select a few questions that go beyond the standard introduction repertoire of "Hello, my name is. . . . , I'm from. . . . , I'm married/single with. . . . , and I work as a. . . . One purpose of guiding questions should be to identify some of the experiences participants have had with residence, with wilderness, with the location, and with the topics explored and the activities planned. A second is to better understand both the motivations and expectations of the participants for attending the program. Some questions may elicit a few sentences, others a word or two. We use the following:

1. How many times have you visited this location and what do you like most about spending time here?

2. When you think of wilderness, what comes to mind? Or, describe a memorable wilderness experience.

3. When was the last time you attended a residence program?

4. What experiences or expertise do you have that can be shared during this residence?

5. I selected this residence program because —.

6. The main thing I hope to learn is —.

7. My biggest contribution to this program may be —.

8. At the moment, my biggest concern is —.

9. Something I hope to "take home" from this program is —.

Then, encourage everyone to share a few responses, being brief and selective. The invitation to be both brief and selective will be a relief to many. It is quite interesting to hear what items people decide to share; inevitably what is not shared at the moment is shared some other time, over dinner for example. The other items become excellent initial conversation starters.

Breaking the Ice

Next, it is useful to structure an activity to increase the personal comfort level of participants with others in the group— for some, residential programs can appear both attractive and threatening. Select an activity that encourages participants to create something in a small group (often less threatening than large groups) rather than discussing some topic together. This could entail deciding upon a group totem and then creating a graphic representation of it. Another possibility could be the creation of environmental sculptures using found objects, à la artist Andy Goldsworthy (n.d.). Or, the group might list various wildlife names appearing in a state map. We especially like this activity, because it is easy to conduct, involves no "touchy feely" stuff, takes little time, and illustrates the significant degree to which wilderness remains part of our social consciousness.

To conduct this activity, the only materials needed are some sheets of poster paper, large colored markers, adhesive tape, and a handful of large state travel maps. If there are participants who drove across state lines to the residence, ask them to share some of the maps used during their journey. As backup, have five to ten different state maps to use as needed.

Ask the entire group to count off. Depending on the number of participants, group size may vary from three to six. The goal is to end with roughly four to five members in each group. Alternatively, consider group composition in advance and make specific assignments. Give each group a different state map, as well as a few sheets of poster paper and some large colored markers for writing. The groups' task is to identify on the map and write on the poster paper all the names of towns, cities, roads, rivers, bridges, and parks, that are named for a species of wildlife (may be plant or animal). Allot groups ten minutes to complete the task.

Once complete, have each group select a spokesperson to share the total number of species identified. It is not uncommon for groups to generate 20–40 unique entries. This task is both enjoyable and educational, providing numerous opportunities to identify and list the magnitude of species found in nature; it also reinforces that society is not totally oblivious to their existence. In addition, this activity provides an opportunity to notice habitat similarities and differences between states, as well as the distribution of species both historically and today. This activity is an extension of one found in the *Project WILD Activity Guide* (1992, p. 20).

COMMUNITY BUILDING

Community building cannot be treated as an afterthought. Given the assignment of roommates and attention to collaborative projects and tasks, groups form quite naturally in a residence setting. But these groups are not necessarily composed of people with a common learning agenda. Efforts to consciously develop learning communities need to be ongoing.

The ideals surrounding learning communities gained prominence in adult education circles when the American Association for Adult Education was formed. To paraphrase one of the architects of the association (Lindeman, 1926/1989), such communities embodied the spirit of an emerging adult education movement: small groups of open-minded adults, drawn together for the purpose of exploration and growth, cognizant of the educative dimension of experience, and guided by nurturing instructors who themselves modeled flexibility and inquisitiveness in thought and acceptance and sincerity in demeanor. For a classic treatment of the educative dimension of experience, refer to Dewey, 1938/1963. Residence programs are excellent vehicles for establishing and realizing the potential embedded in learning communities. When all participants face the same basic challenges there is an equalizing effect and all become colleagues. Participants are able to view each other as resources and references. Program presenters can relax and enjoy their role as a co-inquirer.

Learning communities, once established, are powerful entities. Both challenging and supportive, learning communities are capable of self-direction and self-regulation—changing quite dramatically the teacher-student dynamic surrounding learning in other contexts. For residence planners, establishing learning communities takes skill and a willingness to relinquish some control over the learning agenda. Fortunately, in residence settings, establishing such communities often only takes a nudge, provided a supportive learning climate is established, there exists enthusiasm for the topic, and participants acknowledge they do indeed have something to contribute.

In the previous section, we addressed some initial strategies for establishing a supportive climate. The introductory suggestions —including the sharing of experiences germane to the residence— as well as the ice-breaker activity were included to provide a foundation for forming a learning community. But how does the residence coordinator complete the task? And once in place, how is the learning community maintained throughout the duration of the residence?

Learning communities involve all participants and all participants are expected to contribute in whatever ways are most natural for them. One way participants can contribute is through their willingness to share their expertise in whatever ways may enhance the overall experience of others. We have had participants share their knowledge of specific wilderness areas and lessons learned, their academic or amateur training in a specific area of natural science, their skills as a photographer, musician, or storyteller, to name but a few. Keep in mind, it is not uncommon for participants to feel they have nothing to contribute to the residence and therefore have nothing to contribute to a learning community. This sentiment is quite genuine and is often based upon the perception that only those able to contribute some specific expertise can enhance the experience for others. This feeling is misplaced and should be addressed.

Another way participants can contribute to the formation of learning communities is through attitude. Attitude is everything and as attitude goes, so goes the necessary foundation for dynamic learning. Characteristics of attitude that seem to nurture residential learning communities are the following:

1. acceptance (modeled by program planners and nurtured within the group)

2. willingness to contribute

3. openness to new ideas (not a fixed sense of truth)

4. flexibility and courage

5. appreciation for relationships

We strongly suggest that the intent to nurture learning communities as well as the attitudinal characteristics identified above be included in the introductory session. While the formation of such a community cannot be required, it can still be valued. All members of the program planning committee should model and nurture these attitudinal characteristics. When this happens, generally residence participants begin adopting these characteristics as well.

Groups are as complex as the individuals who compose them, only magnified. But, they are not all that mysterious. Today a great deal of information exists addressing group dynamics and this information may be readily consulted to the advantage of program planners. Basically, establishing a group identity with shared goals depends on the amount of confidence, trust, level of comfort, and degree of support felt by members. While encouraging participants to treat each other with respect and kindness, it is the task of the program planning committee to develop in participants a high degree of trust and confidence.

A TYPICAL DAY

How does a typical day unfold? Every effort is made not to commit a common residence program-planning mistake: information overload. The Achilles heel of many dynamic and content-rich residential programs is packing the agenda with too much information. This is especially unfortunate when programs are conducted in a wilderness area, where outdoor opportunities for solitude and reflection abound. Generally, participants need time—significant amounts of time—to meaningfully integrate and comprehend new information and experiences. Program planners are encouraged to devise instructional strategies and provide opportunities for participants to make mental, physical, and emotional connections to the material covered in the program. For an extensive listing and discussion of instructional strategies for adults refer to Wlodkowski (1999).

We suggest a typical day begin at 7:30 am with breakfast and end at 6:30 pm with dinner. Generally, program sessions should begin at 8:30 am and conclude by 5:00 pm. Prepare box lunches so they can be eaten anytime and anywhere—not requiring the schedule to conform to set meal times. Though this is not always possible, strive to conduct content sessions outdoors. Set aside afternoon sessions for outdoor activities and personal time. Seldom plan evening sessions. Appendix B contains a sample agenda.

There are times when we break or bend these rules. Usually once during the program we have the group gather before sunrise to observe wildlife—generally, this is the time of day animals are most active. We may also plan an evening session for stargazing or for wildlife viewing just prior to sunset—the next best time to observe animals. But, this is rare. Sometimes we organize movie or slide shows in the evenings, and we often provide bonfires and entertainment-often highlighting the musical talents of group members—but these are not required sessions.

Every effort is made to schedule ample time outdoors. Two to four hours of indoor class time should be enough to introduce topics. Remember, the content is primarily a means to assist participants to better understand and appreciate nature, it is not considered an end to be mastered. Then provide time for guided outdoor activities as well as for personal meanderings. In Chapters 5 and 6 we describe how to enhance the wilderness enjoyment of participants concentrating on sauntering and journaling.

Much of the instruction in our residential programs comes from naturalists, broadly defined to include professional biologists, resource managers, educators, and artists, as well as knowl-edgeable amateurs with a passion for nature. Program design determines the number involved, but it is not uncommon to fea-ture three to eight naturalists in a five-day residence. Few of them participate in the entire residence; some provide brief in-struction on site and some join participants in the field. For pre-senters unable to partake fully in the residence, our general rule of thumb is to schedule them for two-hour sessions. This al-lows time for set-up, introductions, instruction, and discussion. Again, devote no more than approximately four hours each day for both on site and field-based formal presentations. The value of unstructured experience in wilderness should not be over-looked.

In addition, to tap into the creative domain of participants, we include some form of craft activity. It might be creating a journal or journal cover. It might be decorating a journal satchel with beadwork or painting a mug. It might be a drawing or a photography assignment. At the beginning of the residence we provide an introductory lesson to the craft and then encourage the development and application of new skills throughout the residence. Participants are often asked to share and comment upon their creations.

WORKING WITH PROGRAM INSTRUCTORS

Because individuals can only digest a given amount of new information—terms, data, ideas—it is generally a very good ap-proach for program instructors to weave new "chunks" of in-formation into the participants' existing knowledge. To do so successfully, instructors need to gauge the understanding of group members, noting the conclusions drawn from these un-derstandings. For example, adults who have spent little time in forest habitats may have little comprehension of the importance of fire in maintaining ecosystem health, often focusing on the negative esthetic of fire-blackened trees. While acknowledging this sense of loss, effective instructors provide a new understand-ing of preservation that encompasses complex processes, not just objects.

Instructors also need to allow time for participants to connect physically to information presented during the program. To better facilitate general understanding and overall comprehension of material, encourage instructors to engage as many of the participants' senses as possible: touching, looking, listening, smelling. Also encourage instructors to use physical exercise to heighten alertness and well being, and to increase energy.

Stress with instructors the importance of assisting participants to "viscerally" connect to a subject. Within wilderness areas, something primeval seems ever present, and encounters with wilderness commonly elicit strong gut reactions. These reactions serve as excellent motivators. Again, refer to Wlodkowski (1999) for some useful tips for motivating adult learners.

Over the years, we have had the good fortune to feature some excellent naturalists and have learned from them a great deal about the ingredients that contribute to successful presentations. In what follows, we address major considerations for effectiveness. As noted in the last chapter, instructors are often selected because they are enthusiastic, creative, and personable. In addition, effective instructors seem to genuinely care about the participants, utilize various methods for presenting information, attend to comprehension and understanding, provide eye contact, and allow time for discussion. While many of the naturalists who present during a residence are specialists, programs may be designed for a rather general audience. Therefore, it is critical presenters and participants establish some common ground for understanding. The remainder of this section explores two instructional strategies common to residence programs in wilderness areas: the slide presentation and the nature field trip.

The Slide Presentation

The most popular medium for residence presentations is the slide show, more recently the PowerPoint presentation. Much can be said for the benefits of this medium for conveying a great deal of information but there are numerous downsides. Slide presentations affect room layout, the behavior of both the presenter and participant, and the delivery of material.

Modifications often need to be made to room layout when slides are used. If tables and chairs are in a circle, they need to be rearranged so all chairs face a wall where a screen is placed and where the presenter stands. When a room is darkened, participants have difficulty seeing both their notebooks and each other. In and of itself this is not a crisis, but such modifications to room layout affect the atmosphere created in the residence and should be acknowledged.

Slide shows also change the behavior of presenters and participants. First there is the set-up of either the slide-projector or the computer. Accepting the maxim that anything that can go wrong with technology eventually will, one must anticipate the worst and be prepared. Still, tension often surrounds working with technology, and this tension is felt by the group. In an attempt to capture a subject adequately, presenters may include far too many slides; once included they generally feel compelled to show each one. In addition, because their focus is directed toward the screen, presenters tend to focus on the slides and not on the group, in some cases actually turning their back to the participants. Turn off the lights, and an instructional methodology is now in place that minimizes learning and maximizes fatigue.

Finally, the slide show format also affects the general delivery of material. Material is often presented in a linear way, from first to last, with few pauses and few deviations. In the case of PowerPoint presentations, there is an opportunity to provide advanced organizers and to move more freely within the presentation (i.e., from slide #6 to slide #14), but not every presenter takes advantage of these opportunities.

So, after experiencing numerous slide shows, what have we learned? We have learned that slide shows and PowerPoint presentations can still be an effective instructional tool, if presenters attend to the following: limit slides, provide an introduction, move around the room, pause often and check the understanding of the group, utilize other visuals, and continually strive to connect to the experience of the group.

Presenters who provide an introduction and link that introduction to what participants have already experienced during the residence, enhance interest. Effective presenters, like effective performers, "work the room," talking to participants conversationally and calling them by name—remember to use the name cards. If presenters have a remote switch to advance slides, they no longer need to position themselves near the computer or projector control and can maneuver freely among participants.

Effective presenters pause during their programs, switch the lights back on, and measure participant understandings. They do so, not by exposing deficiencies of group members, as in asking, "Okay, does everyone understand what's been said thus far—who doesn't?" but by assessing group reactions to specific ideas and topics brought up during the presentation. In this case the presenter might pose a statement and seek a group response, such as, "I mentioned that the idea of wilderness in American culture has changed during the past two centuries. What were some of those changes?" Group members have a chance to respond. Next, and this is where the previous presentation intersects with the experiences and values of the participants, the presenter might ask, "How do your current views about wilderness mesh with the ideas presented?" Group discussion follows. These pauses can be very meaningful for the group and can help maintain interest and engagement in the presentation.

Effective slide show presenters do not rely solely on slides as their visual medium and continually seek creative ways to connect to the experience of the group. We have often witnessed heightened attention when presenters included objects for participants to touch: frozen fish from a nearby lake; the pelt of a wolf; the feathers, beak, skull, and talons of an eagle; and plaster casts of wildlife prints. The more objects people can actually touch, the stronger the impact. It is ideal for objects to be incorporated throughout the presentation and not left for the end when time may be short. The impact of objects is enhanced when there is a conscious effort to connect them to existing knowledge. If sharing the skeleton of a mountain lion, it is effective to compare it to the skeleton of a house cat. This effort provides a powerful bridge connecting previous experiences to new. Illustrate the unfamiliar by including illustrations of the familiar.

Finally, presenters should allow time for discussion. Ideally, this includes attention to "So what?" questions. If the program has been lively and participants are visibly engaged, then discussion can be both meaningful and energizing. Addressing how participants might actually use and apply the information can provide powerful feedback to presenters as well as program planners.

The Nature Field Trip

A second popular medium for residence programming is the field trip. Key qualities of effective nature guides include caring about their audience, utilizing various mediums for presenting information, and attending to comprehension and understanding. In addition, guides need to adjust their programs to the physical fitness level of the group. Perhaps the biggest issue surrounding field trips is logistics.

Fortunately, when residence programs are actually conducted in a wilderness setting, getting to a field trip site (a trailhead, for example) may be no more difficult than gathering outside the residence facility. This is great and at least some of the programmed field trips should begin there. But, all too often, getting to a field trip site involves travel—ideally, the shorter the better.

Getting groups to and from locations is a challenge. Depending on the size of the group, a large bus may be preferred, especially if the featured naturalist is traveling with the group, allowing for mini-presentations and discussions during the trip. But, it is often difficult for large buses to navigate wilderness roads. In addition, when using a bus, all participants are in a sense shackled together, where one goes all are expected to follow. Given differing levels of interest as well as physical conditioning, this can be problematic. Though sometimes useful, our general recommendation is to avoid using large buses. Instead, consider using a few smaller vehicles, such as vans.

Vans have less difficulty navigating back roads, are easier to park, and allow for some options among participants. After a field visit, one van may return to the facility while another may transport a group to different trailhead for a hike. One disadvantage is that featured naturalists cannot use travel time to provide part of their program.

We have found field trips to be most effective when naturalists gauge the fitness level and knowledge base of the group and adjust their program accordingly. This means that program planners need to share with naturalists information about the group. This will help ensure that field trip experiences are enjoyed by all. All group members might be present for the initial part of a guided field trip, then subgroups can be formed according to interest or fitness level.

As recommended for slide show presenters, having visuals and objects to hold and examine greatly enhances field trip experiences. Naturalists who share these items maintain attention. These objects, usually organized and carried in a backpack, can include charts and maps, rocks and bones, feathers and pelts, and visual aids such as models of the earth's interior. They can also include tools used to measure parameters of natural features such as the height and circumference of a tree, the distance across a canyon, or the temperature of a geyser.

We conclude this chapter with a discussion of how we handle the wrap-up session. This may be the most difficult session to manage. Generally, at this point in the residence, participants have developed strong relationships with others and with the setting. Now it is time to return home.

THE WRAP-UP SESSION

Conduct the wrap-up session in a quiet, private, outdoor location if possible. Ideally the location should be easily accessible, preferably within walking distance from the facility. Seek a location where the group can sit comfortably in a circle, and where the sounds, scents, and beauty of nature are rich. Allow at least an hour and weave in a final journaling activity.

As in the case of the program's introduction, the wrap-up session should not be hurried. Often, much is happening at this time and participants are already feeling a strong sense of departure—looking forward to reuniting with family and friends, experiencing some angst about travel, regretting leaving new friends, and feeling a sense of impending loss pertaining perhaps to unrecognized voids filled during the residence. But issues surrounding impending departure are no excuse for not allowing enough time for participants to share their thoughts and emotions about the residence. What was learned? What was its impact? How might this learning alter future choices and behavior? Through verbalization and sharing with others, individuals clarify for themselves what was personally most valuable, and what they want to "remember forever."

An effective wrap-up session might include some of the following elements: a summary of program highlights, guided journaling, and participant sharing. Begin with a review of each day's activities, including wildlife sightings, outstanding hikes, campfires, and key program messages.

While some of the science learned may be unique to the program environment, universal concepts do transfer. Articulate broadly applicable principles relating to specific course content. These include concepts like kinship with other species and the need for habitat preservation for species survival. Survival issues in specific areas might include the presence of invasive species, population pressures, pollution and overharvesting. Similar geologic processes everywhere shape the land and lend greater understanding to the concept of ecosystem. Intact ecosystems are large, complex and must be cooperatively and creatively managed. Biological diversity is one of the hallmarks of a healthy ecosystem. Change is cyclical. Wildlife in its diverse abundance is truly everywhere, yet so is human encroachment. There are not enough green spaces left on the map to afford to lose any. Preservation, conservation, and restoration are needed everywhere. In short, wilderness programs should promote a global land ethic.

Wilson pointed out in *The Future of Life on Earth* (2002), little more than a billion people inhabited the earth in the 1840s

when Thoreau was alive. Today more than 6 billion people inhabit the planet.

> Of these 6 billion people the great majority are very poor; nearly
> one billion exist on the edge of starvation. All are struggling to
> raise the quality of their lives any way they can. That unfortu-
> nately includes the conversion of the surviving remnants of the
> natural environment. Half of the great tropical rainforests have
> been cleared. The last frontiers of the world are effectively gone.
> Species of plants and animals are disappearing a hundred or
> more times faster than before the coming of humanity, and as
> many as half may be gone by the end of this century—The race
> is now on between the techno scientific forces that are destroying
> the living environment and those that can be harnessed to save
> it. We are inside a bottleneck of overpopulation and wasteful
> consumption—in order to pass through the bottleneck, a global
> land ethic is urgently needed. (pp. xxii–xxiii)

Journaling provides time for reflection and can help bring
about closure. One useful journaling activity is to have participants record in their journals everything they can see and everything they are feeling at the moment. This exercise is explained
in more detail in Chapter 6 and helps connect people to the present. Another journal exercise asks participants to reflect on
what has been most significant to them and to record these
thoughts under the headings "Connections with People" and
"Connections with Wilderness."

Finally, we invite participants to share thoughts, photographs, or sketches. Participants should not be forced to share
their feelings about the residence program and experience but
they should have the opportunity to share. We end with a group
photo and goodbyes.

SUMMARY

Be creative, listen to what participants say about the use-
fulness of activities, and provide options. Select activities that
are not treated merely as divergences or escapes from the program but that support the overall purpose of the residence

agenda. Especially in wilderness areas where so many opportunities are available, select activities that allow participants to match their physical endurance as well as their personal interests to differing options, all chosen to support program objectives. Include some form of craft activity and work with instructors to maximize learning. Finally, construct a final session that allows for both closure and transference of new attitudes and behaviors. The next chapter discusses what happens after a program concludes.

CHAPTER 4

Concluding an Event

After the long process of planning a residential program, followed by the exhaustion of delivering the program, it may be tempting to pack it up and think about it all later. While some concluding tasks can and should occur after program planners have had time to rest and reflect, some valuable impressions may be lost if delayed. This chapter addresses debriefing instructors, preparing evaluations, considering requests, expressing thanks, and providing mementos. We conclude with a brief discussion of why, from a planner's perspective, conducting these programs is worthwhile.

INSTRUCTOR DEBRIEFING

Take time to sit down immediately following the program to discuss outcomes with key program staff. While these early impressions may change over time, they are valuable nonetheless. Ask big, open-ended questions, such as "How did it go?" It may be helpful to use a flip chart with two columns: one designated by a + heading (things that were positive and should be retained for the future), the other designated by a delta or change symbol (things that should be changed or done differently in the future). This process should be approached as a brainstorming session, with the goal to generate and capture as many thoughts and opinions as possible, without filtering or editing the results. Differing opinions should be encouraged. Preface the debriefing with a statement to the effect that there are no right or wrong answers, only thoughts to consider. Taking this time to reflect and discuss allows for the sharing of differing perceptions and an important initial read on the success of the residence program. Through sharing with peers, it enables instructors who have been "on" for an extended period of time to relieve themselves of stressful events they may have experienced during the program. Save what was recorded during this session as a tool for future program planning. As such, this is a type of short-term summative, as well as formative evaluation.

EVALUATION

Evaluation strives to answer the basic question—Is the program working? It is typical for people who believe in and care deeply about what they are doing to tend to see their program through rose-colored glasses, to look at cursory feedback and conclude, "Everything is going great!" Engaging seriously in evaluation implies a willingness to look a little deeper. Evaluator Michael Patton described it this way:

> The thing that is challenging about evaluation, when working with people who care deeply about what they do, is the skeptical side that evaluation represents. It is a skeptical perspective. It is a "show me" kind of perspective. It doesn't just acquiesce to passion as a good in and of itself. Caring deeply and intending to do good isn't enough. Evaluation, as a skeptical perspective, asks for some evidence that passion and caring and the strong beliefs that people bring to the things they are doing actually results in the desired good sought. In this sense, evaluation infuses reality-testing into our program world of rose-colored glasses. (Cited in Wiltz, 2001, p. 7)

Patton (1997) defined program evaluation as "the systematic collection of information about the activities, characteristics, and outcomes of programs to make judgments about the program, improve program effectiveness, and/or inform decisions about future programming" (p. 23). For a useful framework for program evaluation specifically for adult audiences refer to Caffarella, 2002.

When evaluation is meant to provide information that can be incorporated into current programming, it is called "formative." Formative evaluation is something program presenters do routinely. It includes observing participant reactions and adjusting to interest and fatigue levels. It includes testing out a new activity. It includes counting the number of people who are attending the "more active" compared to the "less active" hike each day. Formative evaluation is not meant to provide information for decision makers on funding or to assess the program's progress toward goals. It guides the subtle changes, such as solving unanticipated problems or checking participants' progress toward goals—ultimately these things can influence broader program achievement of goals, gauged through summative evaluation.

Summative evaluation does attempt to determine the relative "success" or merit of a program. As such, it is typically done at the end of a program or funding cycle. Summative evaluation reports to an "external" audience who will pass judgment on the program (Scriven, 1994, pp. 1–6).

It may be useful to clarify a few additional terms. Assessment usually refers to the testing of individuals (often cognitive), for the purpose of judging individual performance. This is in contrast to the broader term of evaluation in which individuals may be tested, but the data are analyzed and applied on a collective level. The data are used to judge a program's performance. When a primary program goal is student learning of specific content material, assessments can be useful, although this is not typically a primary goal of adult residential programming.

Outcome is another term that is liberally and diversely applied to evaluation. Outputs, outcomes and impacts all refer to results program planners hope to achieve and measure, or at least document, with evaluation (Wiltz, 2001). Outputs are typically numbers (as in participants), or products (as in books or courses), outcomes are generally broader concepts, such as reactions, affective or cognitive changes that participants take away from the program experience (Wiltz, 2001). It is this accounting for participant reactions, attitudes, and behavior changes after a residential program experience that is often most meaningful to program planners. Likely outcomes of residential experiences include greater sensitivity to the importance of wild places, relationship building, a greater capacity for empathy and tolerance, and a sense of personal renewal. Program impacts are longer-term outcomes, and include those secondary outcomes in which groups are affected or change as a result of the program beyond those who participated. In residential programming for adults in wilderness settings, goals are often stated in terms of broad program impacts such as community building, stewardship for a resource, and a more informed citizenry. While these things may be difficult to measure, if they are deemed important program components they should be considered in the evaluation design. Evaluation should first and foremost be useful. It should answer the questions that those involved want and need to have answered. Patton observed, "It is often better to have weak measurements of important things than to have strong measures of unimportant things" (Cited in Wiltz, 2001, p. 11).

Program planners may choose to wait until participants have had some time to process, reflect, and integrate the residential experience into their daily lives before having them complete an evaluation survey. This will likely require follow-up reminders. A delayed evaluation usually results in a lower return rate than is possible with an onsite evaluation that is an integrated part of conclusion and wrap-up. Sachetello-Sawyer, et al. (2002) suggested distributing a basic evaluation form at the end of a program, followed by a phone interview six to eight weeks after the program targeting program transference measures. They feel this delay allows time for a more accurate assessment of program transference, or application of what has been learned.

When it comes to program evaluation, we do a few things. We encourage feedback throughout the program. Approximately two weeks following a program we mail a written evaluation to all participants. See Appendix C for a sample. A group photograph and a personal letter accompany the evaluation. In the letter we express appreciation for their contributions to the residence and announce dates for next year's program.

PARTICIPANT CONTACT LISTS

Program planners may want to provide a list of program attendees and their contact information to all participants. This can be done at the end of the course, or soon after it concludes. Such a list facilitates future ties and continued relationship building should individuals so desire. Ask permission first, and include a disclaimer that the list is for the personal use of participants and will not be distributed for any other purposes.

INFORMATION FOLLOW-UPS

There is a good chance that over the course of an extended residential experience a long list of things planners offered to do for participants will accumulate. These might include adding participants to a mailing list, tracking down an elusive piece of information, or sending participants a copy of a professional article. Respond to these things in a timely fashion. It will be greatly appreciated.

THANK YOU NOTES

Many people work hard to make a residential program successful. Be sure and take the time to thank them. Handwritten notes are best. Send these to everyone who helped with program-related tasks. Because planners are continuously present during the program, and have the opportunity to establish relationships with all participants, they will likely hear more feedback than an instructor who may only join the group for an hour or two. Be sure and share this information with instructors. Unless program planners supervise presenters or work very closely with them, they should consider using thank you notes as an opportunity to coach guest instructors on their performance. Be explicit about strengths, tactfully offer suggestions where needed, and offer specific participant comments as supporting evidence whenever possible. When done well, this is a welcome opportunity for instructors and fosters their professional growth. Positive relationships built with instructors helps retain good instructors for future programs.

MEMENTOS

It is a nice addition if a memento of the program can be sent to each participant. This might be as simple as a group photo, including names. Other mementos that have been produced by our residence participants and shared with all have included a "documentary" style video/photo montage on disk, and an electronic scrapbook, complete with photos, text (including creative writings by students), and music recorded during the residence program. Often individual interests generate such products and they evolve somewhat spontaneously during and after a course. Encourage and facilitate the sharing of such projects. These allow participants to relive and continue to process this significant event.

COMMUNICATE THE VALUE OF
YOUR PROGRAM

Once the residential program concludes, share the experiences with others. Write about the program for the popular press or a professional journal. Present ideas at a conference, develop a website, and start a listserv or bulletin board to facilitate sharing ideas with others in the field.

WHY DO IT—A PLANNER'S PERSPECTIVE

Planning an event, conducting an event, concluding an event—it is a lot of work. Why embark on such a journey? It all comes down to an understanding that ultimately evolves into a conviction that these programs are an incredibly effective method for moving agendas and changing lives. When people become

intimate with wild lands, they become a more informed citizenry with a strong sense of stewardship for these places—and
by extension for wildness everywhere. When this happens, it is
possible to achieve a global land ethic and all that might imply.
That motivates. When adults expand their realm of interaction
and become intimate with other adults, they stretch and grow
and learn new, more creative, tolerant, in short, healthier ways
of being that are not easily accessed otherwise. To see these
transformations, to be integral to this kind of growth, is another
powerful motivator.

The effort of the program planner is not altogether altru-
istic. Program planners often gain more than they give. Planners
are co-beneficiaries of the experiences they create. Do it for the
environment, do it for others, do it for the personal satisfaction.

Edward Abbey was a respected American writer noted as a
crusader for wilderness. Passionate, often irreverent, Abbey pre-
scribed personal time in wilderness as a remedy for burnout.

> Do not burn yourselves out. Be as I am—a reluctant enthusiast . . .
> a part-time crusader, a half-hearted fanatic. Save the other half
> of yourselves and your lives for personal pleasure and adventure.
> It is not enough to fight for the West; it is even more important
> to enjoy it. While you can. While it's still there.
>
> So get out there and hunt and fish and mess around with your
> friends. Ramble out yonder and explore the forests, encounter
> the GRIZZ, climb the mountains, bag the peaks, run the rivers,
> breathe deep of that yet sweet and lucid air, sit quietly for a while
> and contemplate the precious stillness, that lovely, mysterious
> and awesome space.
>
> Enjoy yourselves, keep your brain in your head and your head
> firmly attached to your body, the body active and alive, and I
> promise you this much: I promise you this one sweet victory over
> our enemies, over those desk-bound men with hearts in a safe
> deposit box and their eyes hypnotized by desk calculators. I
> promise you this: you will outlive the bastards. (Van Matre,
> 1983, p. 57)

Program planners of residential wilderness experiences for
adults truly can have the best of both worlds—the realization of
compelling and imperative professional goals, as well as multi-

ple opportunities for personally transforming and rejuvenating experiences.

SUMMARY

Chapters 2, 3, and 4 addressed many of the challenges program planners face when planning, conducting, and concluding residential adult education programs in wilderness areas. A genuine sense of humility and awe for all life forms that inhabit the planet earth certainly helps compensate for all the efforts such programming requires. As noted above, the benefits to participants, wilderness areas and to the program planners themselves are vast and varied. At the end of the day, such programs are capable of impacting the lives of participants in dramatic ways and altering forever attitudes toward other species and wild places.

The next two chapters touch on strategies that attempt to enhance the experiences of program participants in wilderness areas and to assist in capturing those moments for future use. Chapter 5 "Sauntering" covers a variety of techniques for engaging the senses in the discovery of wild places. Chapter 6 "Journaling" introduces methods for thinking about and recording time spent in wilderness areas.

CHAPTER 5

SaPuntpPering

I have met with but one or two persons in the course of my life
who understood the art of Walking, that is, of taking walks,—
who had a genius, so to speak, for sauntering. (Thoreau, 1862/
1977, p. 71)

The heartbeat of the program is found in wilderness.
Whether approached joyfully or tentatively, time spent in "wild"
surroundings is what these residence programs uniquely provide. Recognize the depth of feelings elicited by the setting and
continually seek ways to enhance the individual-wilderness relationship.

This chapter explores sauntering as a meaningful approach
to experience wilderness. It begins by briefly sharing Thoreau's
view of sauntering and then discusses some of the attitudinal dimensions of sauntering, including being fully alert to surroundings. Next, comes a discussion of why some participants benefit
from a little reprogramming of their minds and bodies so as to
fully engage their senses when experiencing both new and familiar surroundings. We also present a relaxation technique
found helpful to facilitate this process. An illustration follows
of a group of professionals who have mastered the sauntering
attitude: nature photographers. Finally there is a discussion of
how we organize hikes, their purpose, and how we attempt to
help participants enjoy hiking—themes addressed include recognizing limitations, dressing appropriately and using appropriate gear, and avoiding unnecessary risks.

DEVELOPING A SAUNTERING ATTITUDE

In an earlier chapter, Thoreau was introduced as was his instructive essay *Walking*. Thoreau enjoyed walking for its physical benefits as well as for its effect on his general state of being. He loved to saunter and generally viewed walking as an adventure; we agree. Here, the term *saunter* refers to both an attitude and an activity. A sauntering attitude is one that views the land and other species respectfully. For Thoreau, sauntering was foremost a sort of crusade, a going forth and a *reconquering* of the land for natural purposes—land and nature were to be appreciated and experienced as places that support a magnitude of life forms (1862/1977). Thoreau had formulated a land ethic a century before Aldo Leopold questioned the economic value human beings assigned to land and popularized the view of land as a biotic mechanism.

Sauntering also heightened the senses, allowing individuals to experience life more completely. In his famous essay *Walden* (1854/1971), Thoreau shared the main reason for his Walden Pond experiment in which he lived for two years in a modest cabin constructed entirely by himself:

> I wished to live deliberately, to front only the essential facts of life, and see if I could not learn what it had to teach, and not, when I came to die, discover that I had not lived. I did not wish to live what was not life, living is so dear; nor did I wish to practice resignation, unless it was quite necessary. I wanted to live deep and suck out all the marrow of life. (pp. 90–91)

Sauntering allowed Thoreau to touch, to examine, to experience other life forms, and to constantly learn new things. As noted above, the purposes that guided these walks were really twofold: one was to celebrate the natural world, the world little touched by human beings, and the other was to experience the natural world humbly, as a student. But to truly learn from surroundings, Thoreau argued, individuals must be fully present and fully engaged.

Being in the Present

Perhaps it is easier to build a case for living in the present when individuals accept Thoreau's view of the preciousness of each moment, that life, indeed, is far too short. Thoreau encouraged individuals to courageously accept that life passes quickly, and because of this, not to waste time and not to postpone living a meaningful existence. But, living in the present can be difficult. Being in the present necessitates some deprogramming and some new ways of living.

Being in the present means being fully aware of both internal and external happenings: breathing as well as surroundings. It is not enough for residential planners to argue the merits of experiencing the present and then commence activities intended to engage the senses. They must first accept that for some program participants, experiencing wholly the present may be rather foreign and may actually be challenging. Therefore, teach some simple relaxation awareness exercises, then encourage participants to practice these each day.

Reprogramming the Body

An extreme example of being fully acute to the present is the physiological fight/flight response to threatening situations. Time seems to slow and senses are heightened by a rush of adrenalin. Some individuals react this way in wilderness especially where large carnivores are present. Few of these people actually register for wilderness programs; but some do, either cautiously expanding their horizons or dutifully accompanying a significant other. Most of our participants are not at all threatened by wilderness; they seek it and are energized by it. However, people may still benefit from exercises that promote relaxed awareness.

For many adults whose basic needs for survival are met, daily living becomes rather routine; the senses become less acute because they are not called upon to function at a keen level.

Habitual ways of deciphering surroundings are adopted and the senses are naturally dulled. As residence planners, acknowledge this, and without resorting to intentionally placing participants in threatening situations, attempt to do something about it. Relaxation and conscious attention to how the body performs can offer a pleasant way to enhance the senses. Fortunately, many relaxation programs are available—t'ai chi, meditation, yoga, and the Alexander Technique, to name but a few. If time permits during the residence, it is useful to include a relaxation program as an early-riser optional activity, much like a sunrise hike. This option has been included in some of the residential programs offered by Michael during the University of Wyoming Mountain Folk School.

When relaxation activities are optional, not all will gain their benefits. Therefore, introduce the exercises to everyone, then encourage individuals to repeat them each day. This need not require a lot of time and extra equipment. A simple approach that can be completed in a few minutes either inside or preferably outside is a modified form of the Alexander Technique, developed in the late 19th century by Frederick Mathias Alexander. Used widely by dancers and actors, the Alexander Technique involves simple movements, breathing, and guided imagery to create a sense of aware relaxation. These exercises stress both relaxation and sensation—the sensation of being in touch with one's entire body.

Make every effort to clarify the intent of the relaxation activity and to suggest the benefits of participation, but never demand that people participate. Suggest to participants that experiencing a wilderness setting—like experiencing any setting—is greatly improved if the sense organs are finely tuned. Because humans develop the means to decipher their surroundings with minimal conscious effort, much living is experienced only partially. In addition, Richard Craze, an Alexander Technique teacher, has suggested that the human body has not yet adapted to modern living and that children use their bodies much more naturally than adults. Craze (2001) observed that numerous creations of civilized life, such as the design of most chairs, actually contribute to stress and tension by creating unnatural body alignments. Some deprogramming of the mind as well as the body seem essential for producing natural ways of being. When human beings do not feel threatened, there exists little biological need to alert the senses. Given that sensory awareness is fundamental to fully appreciate surroundings, residential programs should intentionally awaken the senses. Instructions follow.

There need be no "correct" way to conduct the initial relaxation activity but emphasis should be placed on developing a harmonious interaction between breathing, simple movements, and guided imagery. According to Craze, the basic building blocks of the Alexander Technique are 1) to allow the neck to be free; 2) to let the head go forward and up; and 3) to allow the back to lengthen and widen (p. 26). This posture facilitates slow, deep, and full breathing. Encourage participants to close their eyes, relax (but stay alert), stand tall (straightening and widening their backs and concentrating on posture), imagine their heads floating forward and up, and to stand in a comfortable and relaxed "athletic" position. Joints should be loose, legs should be spread about shoulder-width apart, and feet should be placed firmly on the ground. From this position, while maintaining slow, deep, full breaths, focus on each sense organ through guided imagery.

First, ask participants to imagine they are looking at a common object found in nature; it could be a tree, a bird, etc. Ask them to see it as part of a more elaborate setting. Then ask the group to slowly concentrate on the subject and increase their gaze, looking ever closer at the subject, seeing details (imagining them if need be), and then to view the subject from different angles—from above, from below, from behind. Finally, ask them to slowly return to their initial point of concentration, their initial gaze. Do this for all the sense organs, selecting a sound (such as a gurgling brook), selecting a smell (such as sage or Ponderosa Pine), selecting a taste (such as a blueberry), and selecting an object to touch and feel (such as a feather or an animal's fur pelt). Ask participants to silently identify what they are hearing, smelling, tasting, and touching and then to magnify and increase their sensations.

This is all there is to it. Have the group slowly return their concentration to the present, to continue standing comfortably erect, to continue breathing slowly, fully, and deeply, to now be aware of sounds and smells all around them, to feel the ground, to taste what they concentrated on earlier and finally, to slowly open their eyes. Give them a few moments to reconnect with where they are standing and then encourage participants to apply the same techniques throughout the day, especially when hiking. If participants wish to explore the Alexander Technique further, have a few copies of Craze's book on hand to share.

Generally, you do not need to repeat the activity. Encourage participants to spend some time at the beginning of each day repeating this or some other relaxation and sense-enhancing activity on their own—this could be shortly after they wake, while they are waiting for a shower, or before breakfast. If they find the exercise useful, encourage them to continue the routine when they return home.

SAUNTERING AND NATURE PHOTOGRAPHERS

In continuing to develop a sauntering attitude, it is helpful to include tips from successful nature photographers. These individuals make a living patiently observing nature. By examining photographs by Charles Campbell, Tim Fitzharris, Weldon Lee, John Shaw, and others, and sharing their writings, numerous suggestions are provided for fully experiencing wilderness. These include becoming a friend of wilderness, viewing surroundings purposefully and from many perspectives, attending to detail and patterns, developing an appreciation for little things, and being patient and willing to become students of nature.

Being a friend to and of wilderness begins with adopting a respectful attitude toward other species. Impress upon program participants the importance of neither intentionally or carelessly destroying, nor disrupting an animal's home, or approaching wildlife too closely. In *Walking Softly in the Wilderness*, John Hart (1998) acknowledged, "hardly a wilderness anywhere is free of recreational scars" (p. 4). But this is no excuse for exacerbating the situation. Walk carefully and considerately. As for photographing wildlife, nature photographers concur that a comfortable working distance be maintained so as not to disrupt behavior. Far too often careless (and reckless) "picture takers" aggressively pursue wildlife in the hope of taking a "trophy" photograph. Author and photographer Weldon Lee cautioned (1996), "No photograph is worth more than the well-being of [the] subject" (p. 9).

Nature photographer and author Charles Campbell (1994) has encouraged individuals to slow their pace when in wilderness and to really focus on surroundings:

> Take time to see beyond the obvious. Scan your surroundings for things that you find interesting and believe worthwhile sharing with others. Also look for more abstract images filled with interesting shapes, patterns, textures, and colors. Something will eventually grab your attention and draw you in for closer scrutiny. (pp. 126–127)

Campbell further suggested that nature explorers get into the habit of altering the direction of looking. In addition to looking forward, look up, down, and back; it is amazing what interesting and unexpected commonplace objects will come into view. Adopting these approaches to experiencing and reflecting upon wilderness are major themes woven throughout our residence programs. One of the unexpected pleasures of outdoor photography, noted by Campbell,

> . . . is that it develops a keener vision that deepens our appreciation and understanding of the natural world. In fact, each of us has a unique and valid way of seeing the world. With this unique vision comes the opportunity to make photographic images that bear our unique stamp as individuals. (1994, pp. 11–12)

As Tim Fitzharris suggested, become more aware of the little things, nature's miniature world. Acquaint residence participants with nature up close and intimate. A small magnifying glass held in front of a flower or an insect, or used to closely observe lichen on a rock or the bark of a tree, often produces amazement and awe. Nature's patterns, the beauty of complimentary colors so delicately arranged, often go unnoticed. Nature photographers are acutely aware of this world, and often use close-up lenses to produce "magical" images. Fitzharris shared some wonderful images in the *National Audubon Society Guide to Nature Photography* (2003). In that work he observed, "Nature's miniature world is home to some of the most beautiful and easily photographed subjects—dew drops, wildflowers, butterflies, spiders" (p. 24).

Successful nature photographers also demonstrate a phenomenal degree of patience. There is often a big difference in the quality of photographs taken hurriedly and those taken with control and finesse. The later are dependent upon technical expertise, sensitivity to composition, and the ability to sit patiently—to wait for a subject to appear, for clouds to develop or disappear, for a storm to settle or escalate, for just the right light. Encourage those who want to more fully experience wilderness to study the work of successful nature photographers.

Becoming a good nature photographer also requires becoming a more conscientious student of nature—becoming an amateur naturalist. John Shaw, a very successful nature photographer and author, sees a strong connection between knowledge of nature, compassion for all living things, concern about wildlife, and taking better nature photos. He wrote, "Only after we have let our minds and eyes deal intimately with the abundance of natural marvels around us should we attempt to photograph them" (2000, p. 6). As Thoreau expressed in a passage referred to earlier, a major reason why he took up residence near Walden Pond was to become more informed about nature—to learn what nature had to teach. Like Thoreau, any individual can become a keen observer and student of nature. All it takes is an attitude of curiosity and a few simple tools. These tools, according to naturalist author Stephen Whitney, only need be a notebook, pen or pencil, a pair of binoculars, and perhaps a hand lens (1997). One more thing, nature photographers tend to really enjoy hiking and spending time outdoors.

ENJOYING A WALK

The physical activity of wilderness sauntering improves both mental and physical health. The link between exercise and general feelings of mental, emotional, and physical well-being is well established. But sauntering need not be equated with extensive exercise. Few people aspire to walk as long, as far, and as often as Thoreau. Sauntering of the mind can also occur sitting behind a desk, observing surroundings, and reflecting upon those observations.

Having said this, during a residence program sauntering typically entails some form of physical exercise, usually walking outdoors. As suggested earlier, at least half of each day should take place outdoors. Provide hiking options. While we recognize the benefits of physical exercise, our focus is not primarily the hiking. Our focus is the meandering, the adventure, and the opportunity to experience the unexpected. During these outings, chat with participants about what they see and might expect to see, enjoy exploring habitats, and enjoy the expressions of delight, wonder, and comprehension on faces. We also enjoy the hiking and the exercise. At the end of a field session, when time permits and if some participants are eager to continue hiking, encourage them to do so. This is one reason to spend time during the introduction session familiarizing participants with local trails and safety. Sometimes we join them on these spontaneous excursions.

Some readers may not enjoy walking—some of our program participants begin a residence with the same attitude. But, as program planners, one of your major tasks is to help individuals enjoy the outdoors and that generally means helping them enjoy hiking. And to enjoy hiking, individuals need to know their limitations, dress appropriately, use appropriate gear, and avoid taking unnecessary risks.

Knowing Personal Limitations

A major part of becoming physically fit is knowing personal limitations. Program participants need not walk as far as Thoreau to enjoy being outdoors, but they need to get started and to gauge their abilities realistically. A half-mile walk can produce fatigue for overweight and out of shape adults. Add rough terrain and elevation gains, and a half-mile hike becomes even more strenuous. When encouraging more time outdoors, assess the fitness level of the group and set realistic expectations. Inquire about the current physical activity level of all participants. When asked about fitness, there is a tendency for some people to share their highest level of fitness for the past few years. Be more interested in participants' level of activity for the past month. Resist appearing judgmental. If participants feel it is okay to be truthful, they tend to share more honest and reliable information.

Have group members select walking distances that should take no more than 20 minutes to complete beyond what they are used to. Less active outings are generally under a mile long, allowing participants to sample the joy of being out of doors with minimal physical exertion; more active outings often cover three to four miles. Allow participants to pause as needed, enabling them to absorb some of the sights, sounds, and smells nature richly provides. As explored in the next chapter, schedule periodic journal breaks. At these times, participants can sit, intentionally focus on their surroundings, and write.

Finding pleasure in spending time out of doors should be a primary residence goal. This is something many participants learn to enjoy during a program and continue to enjoy once they return home. Participants are most likely to enjoy their time outdoors when they only need stretch their endurance a little bit at a time. When monitored to avoid overexertion and encouraged, participants steadily increase the hiking distance they are able to cover comfortably. To help this occur, encourage participants to note in their journals the distance covered each day, the amount of time a hike lasted, and the degree of fatigue felt at the end of the hike. If fatigued, encourage participants to cut back on their hiking distance the next day. If not fatigued, the next day they can gradually increase their hiking distance. When determining the right distance for a hike, generally less is best. Ideally, participants end each day's hike with some energy in reserve, stored up to draw upon the next day.

Again and again, time spent hiking is identified by our program participants as one of the transforming parts of their residence experience. Repeat resident participants often return in better condition than the previous year.

How well individuals can condition themselves is remarkable, if they approach physical activities intelligently and deliberately. Slow, steady, patient progress is fundamental. Michael has had success preparing joggers to run a marathon (26 miles, 385 yards) even when their initial running commitment and distance were quite modest—perhaps running three times a week, with their longest run being 3 miles. In eight months these joggers were prepared to run and complete the marathon. Though it might take nearly three months for these joggers to go from a 9-mile running week to an 18 or 20-mile running week, it only took another month or so for them to complete a 30-mile week. At this point in their training, they were able to cover, without excessive exertion, 10 miles during a single run. Over the next four months, these runners increased their weekly mileage to 50 miles, with long runs approaching 22–23 miles. As in the case of increasing hiking distance, there was nothing mysterious about these physical accomplishments. They were accomplished primarily because of commitment, consistency, and steady progress.

Dressing Appropriately and
Selecting Appropriate Equipment

Nothing dampens a pleasurable hike more than becoming chilled or chafed, carrying a daypack that is too heavy, or developing a blister. For this reason, participants should receive a list of suggested clothing and equipment in advance of a residence. See Appendix B for an example.

When in wilderness, "Expect the unexpected!" For example, in August, temperatures in Yellowstone can fluctuate from slightly above freezing to highs in the 80s at midday. As is true throughout the Rocky Mountain region, it can snow in Yellowstone at any time, and afternoon thunderstorms can be severe and occur with little warning.

Discuss proper wilderness clothing and equipment early in

the program. Participants should be alerted to just how unpredictable wilderness weather is. Stress that certain fabrics are much better at withstanding the rise and fall of outdoor temperatures than others. Encourage participants to dress comfortably in layers: synthetic t-shirt next to the skin, synthetic shirt, light fleece pullover, and some form of light jacket that can withstand both wind and rain. Hat, gloves, and an extra dry pair of wool or synthetic socks should be packed for easy retrieval. For those who ignored the clothing list included in the packet and bring nothing but cotton clothing, we do our best to accommodate—loaning items or directing them to one of the local gift shops where synthetic clothing is often available for purchase. Returning program participants do not make the same mistake twice.

In addition, make participants aware of the ebb and flow of core body temperature when sauntering outdoors. As participants exert increasing amounts of energy while hiking, their core body temperature rises and they sweat. They need to adjust their clothing to these increases in exertion; that is why some of the better jackets are ventilated with mesh under the armpits or under a flap on the back. Then there are those moments when participants stop hiking, to complete a journal activity perhaps. With little physical exertion core body temperature drops and individuals feel chilled. Hat, gloves, and synthetic socks are excellent body temperature regulators. Covering extremities as needed can help fine-tune temperature regulation and comfort.

When participants are outdoors encourage them to wear synthetic and wool clothing and to avoid wearing fabrics that hold onto moisture, get heavy when wet, and are major chill producers. As for appropriate equipment, from hiking shoes to backpacks, advise participants to try them before coming to the residence and only to bring what has been proven comfortable and useful.

Require participants to bring a lightweight, comfortable daypack. The pack should have both a waist and chest strap, distributing weight comfortably. The pack should be large enough to minimally hold a rain poncho, wind jacket, warm hat, gloves, and an extra pair of wool or synthetic socks. If a lightweight fleece pullover is not being worn then it should also be included in the pack. The pack should also have mesh pockets on the sides for carrying at least one water bottle. Carrying a small first-aid kit is also encouraged. Include at least some blister bandages, tape, tweezers (for removing slivers), small scissors (for cutting tape), and antibiotic ointment (for cuts and scrapes). A pocket-knife comes in handy. Seldom do these packs when loaded need to weigh much more than ten pounds. Also encourage participants to bring binoculars and to wear them, strapped around the neck, whenever they are outdoors.

Avoid Unnecessary Risks

This final section goes beyond comfort and deals directly with safety. When hiking in wilderness settings, anticipating and remaining vigilant to the unpredictable is always a good way to proceed. Staying on marked trails, being attentive to the placement of the sun and to the general direction a trail is heading, having a trail map and compass, keeping an eye on the time, having some extra clothing, carrying a flashlight, are all recommended.

When outdoors we have one general rule we share with program participants where safety is concerned. If going forward on a trail stresses an animal, if continuing a hike late in the day means returning in the dark, if a trail crosses a river of unknown depth, if continuing on a poorly marked trail might mean becoming lost, if crossing a hillside means traversing loose rocks, do not take that risk. There is plenty to experience in the out-of-doors that does not require taking unnecessary risks.

Be familiar with the trails you choose to use. But, sometimes opportunities occur and an unfamiliar trail becomes suddenly attractive. In this situation, learn as much about the trail as possible and proceed cautiously, monitoring closely distance and time. Though this is an exception to our rule, sometimes exceptions are made. Know when to make the exceptions and when not to.

Safety in wilderness is based on a little common sense and

Basic Emergency Equipment

- map
- flashlight
- wool hat
- matches in a waterproof container
- 8-inch highway safety flare (excellent fire starter)

- compass
- emergency food
- space blanket

- first aid kit
- water
- bear spray (when in bear country)
- iodine tablets for treating additional water

- radio
- extra clothing

Figure 5.1 Basic Emergency Equipment

a lot of appreciation for wildlife and their surroundings. When program participants respect wildlife and their home environments, they will not tromp carelessly, thoughtlessly, and dangerously through their habitats.

GENERAL SAFETY GUIDELINES FOR WILDERNESS PROGRAMS

The primary concern with regard to health issues in wilderness areas is the distance to advanced medical care. Even programs that include little activity and do not venture far from developed areas may take place in areas where access to advanced medical care may be significantly delayed. Therefore, it is imperative that a proactive stance be adopted with regard to safety. As noted above, this means avoiding unnecessary risks.

A good policy is to always travel in groups. Even minor mishaps can become life threatening when there is no help available. If someone even briefly leaves the group, they should notify another. Leaders should regularly count heads to make sure everyone is present. At least one member of any group should carry the basic emergency equipment noted in Figure 5.1.

Leaders should be trained in driver safety, wilderness medicine, and the use of portable radios. Additionally, leaders should be aware of the weather forecast and any other special information. They should maintain an awareness of landmarks, general direction of travel, length of daylight remaining, and health and comfort status of group members. Leaders should request that all group members monitor themselves, and keep the leader informed of any problems. Despite the combined efforts of all involved, wilderness programs entail some inherent risks, many of which are associated with physical activity in high altitude mountainous terrain.

PROVIDING TREATMENT WHEN NECESSARY

In spite of the best preventative steps, situations may arise necessitating the treatment of illness or injury. To be prepared for this eventuality, emergency procedures should be in place. Determine in advance of the course the person in the group having the highest level of medical training and experience in wilderness settings. This person is the primary first aid provider and should be in charge of emergency medical treatment. A group manager, the person with the next most experience, is responsible for the healthy members of the group during an emergency, and should also be available to assist the primary first aid provider as necessary and to the extent of his or her training. Create in advance an emergency medical response flowchart detailing procedures for major as well as minor health incidents. All medical incidents should be documented, including near misses, as these can be instructive for prevention.

SUMMARY

In this chapter sauntering was discussed as a meaningful approach to experience wilderness. As noted at the beginning of the chapter, strengthening the individual-wilderness relationship is what drives our residence programs. By stressing a sauntering attitude and scheduling lots of time outdoors, we strive to increase comfort level and appreciation for wild places. Both the attitudinal and physical dimensions of sauntering were explored and techniques to assist program participants to experience wilderness environments alertly, meaningfully, and safely were discussed. Sauntering was also explored from the perspective of professional nature photographers—a group who seem to have mastered this art. We concluded with some suggestions for helping residence participants enjoy hiking. These suggestions included recognizing physical limitations, dressing appropriately and using appropriate gear, and avoiding unnecessary risks. In the next chapter we discuss journaling as a compelling reflective and recording tool.

CHAPTER 6

Journaling

Through our work with young people and adults participating in residential programs, we have developed a strong commitment to journaling. In this chapter we define journaling, discus the benefits of journaling, make some specific suggestions for creating journals and facilitating journaling, and finally, provide some sample assignments as well as examples of student writing.

WHAT IS JOURNALING?

The term *journaling* has been widely applied in diverse educational settings for a multitude of useful purposes. Most often, this term applies to one of three things: a diary of daily events, a field journal or scientific record, which might include statistics relative to temperature and precipitation, or a creative journal, in which directed writing assignments encourage creative, original thought. For our purposes, the creative journal is the best match, though ours is at heart an inclusive sort of journal that might include bits of other types as well. It is, in essence, a simple but highly effective tool for deepening perception. To read more about creative journaling refer to Ferra (1994) and Hinchman (1991, 1997).

Thoreau was a journal keeper. In his words, the naturalist's keen eye is recognized. To him, a meadow was much more than a sea of undifferentiated green—rather, it was an intricate profusion of plants and animals whose forms and habits he knew well and reveled in describing (Thoreau, 1849/1977). Many writers and artists are journal keepers. The pages of their journals are where they capture the bare-boned essence of things. It is where they return for bits and pieces, images and inspiration. Their journals provide glimpses into the creative process. Great artists and writers are known through their finished works, but their sketchbooks and journals often reveal a roving, observant eye.

WHY JOURNALING?

Author Annie Dillard said,

> All those things for which we have no words are lost. The mind—the culture—has two little tools, grammar and lexicon: a decorated sand bucket and a matching shovel. With these we bluster about the continents and do all the world's work. With these we try to save our very lives. (1982, p. 99)

Residential programs are inherently rich and multifaceted. While this is a good thing, the potential exists to overload people. Each person has a point of saturation beyond which little can be absorbed. Imagine being in an unfamiliar and disorienting learning environment that demands focused attention 10 to 12 hours a day. Add to this a cadre of unfamiliar instructors, an unfamiliar peer group, dormitory sleeping arrangements, and a loss of control over what and when you will eat. Breaks are essential. The creative journal serves as a vehicle to catch insights and ideas that might otherwise be lost. Images and events pass through the journal keeper and settle on the pages. Well positioned and liberally applied throughout a residential experience, journaling can provide a mosaic of still points for reflection and rejuvenation in what can be an overstimulating and physically exhausting landscape. Journaling provides a time and place to process a barrage of new experiences, knowledge, and emerging conclusions concerning the personal significance of events. It encourages people to be fully aware and present. As discussed in the previous chapter, to become better observers and recorders of both external and internal landscapes, individuals first need to be fully present—stopping and noticing what is going on in the setting as well as what is going on inside themselves. Journaling encourages thinking beyond the facts. While the juxtaposition of seemingly unrelated bits may seem strange at first, when looked back upon, patterns float to the surface, helping make sense of the whole and bringing the experience into sharper focus. Directed journaling can draw out the personal connections that have lasting meaning—the realizations that can turn an enjoyable experience into a life-transforming one.

Journals can be very personal and should always be private—to be shared only if participants choose to. Creative journals should never be graded. When working within the formal K-12 educational system, Ellen specifically requests that teachers honor this premise. If it is necessary for instructors to assess written work during a residency, select a few assignments for this purpose, and make it known to the journal-keepers in advance those assignments that must be copied from journals and submitted for a grade. An assessment rubric should be explained prior to these assignments. As we have mentioned previously, to gain the most from a residential experience, it is essential that participants feel safe: not only physically, but also from the personal judgment of others, as well as from academic judgment and pressures.

CREATING JOURNALS

The first step toward effectively facilitating journaling is selecting or creating a journal that will be durable, practical, and aesthetically appealing. The journal, including its cover and construction, should communicate in all ways that it is something of value, something that will be a lasting memento of the experience at the very least—perhaps something that will become even more enduring and meaningful over time. The journal should not be too large to travel easily in a backpack or satchel. A dimension of approximately nine by six inches typically works well. Blank pages are preferable, as lined pages have a deadening influence. Pages should be heavy enough to work equally well for writing, sketching, and possibly watercolor. The journal should be well bound for durability. Spiral bindings work well, as they allow books to lie flat which is conducive to sketching. A stiff backing is essential for writing in field settings. Shop around—artist's sketchbooks as well as crafter's scrapbooks work well and can be obtained in large department stores relatively inexpensively.

Journals should be distributed near the beginning of a residence program. Once each person has been presented with a journal, and its purpose has been discussed, journals should be personalized in some way. Rather than have residence participants write their names on the covers, we often have them create a collage of images. This begins the process of personal investment that adds value, makes it easier to tell journals apart, sparks creativity, and helps group members get to know one another better.

To make collage journal covers, provide an assortment of magazines from which to tear or cut images. While some individuals prefer the precision of cutting, encourage them to experiment with tearing. Tearing in different directions will vary the soft-edged effect. Also, there is something wonderfully freeing about ripping pages out of magazines and tearing with complete abandon. It seems to loosen inhibitions and foster creativity. From the time children are first able to grasp things firmly with their hands, often they are admonished not to engage in this destructive behavior—yet any parent of a young child will confirm how tempting and satisfying it seems to be! Overlapping images create an attractive collage when glued directly onto journal covers. Simple glue sticks work fine. Include magazines that feature natural images, especially of the environment in which the residence program is being conducted. Once designs are complete, overlay covers with clear contact paper. Allow for a margin of approximately one-half inch. Fold the margin under so that it adheres to the back of the cover on the top, bottom, and outer edges. Clip the corners off before folding in the margins for a neat fit.

When covers are finished, an effective group activity is having participants share their work by explaining why they selected the images they did. This encourages self-disclosure and helps individuals get to know each other better.

ENCOURAGING WRITING

The best way to encourage writing is to model writing. Program leaders should never ask residence participants to write without simultaneously engaging in the activity themselves. Following an assignment, encourage participants to share their written work, but never require it. Program leaders may choose to share their own writing, but they need not be first and need not share every time. Be a good listener. Offer feedback. This might be as simple as sincerely thanking the reader for sharing. It might include drawing a comparison, or singling out something particularly interesting. When participants are observed smiling or laughing as they work on assignments, share and discuss this phenomenon. Encourage imperfection. Teach that the creative process is an end in and of itself—creative work is play. Teacher, artist, and author Julia Cameron said this about imperfection and creativity in *The Artist's Way*:

> [My mother] once filled out a questionnaire that asked, "Can you sing?" by answering "Yes. Average." My mother's "yes, average" voice sang "Turra Lurra Lurra." Her "average" piano skills gave us the "Blue Danube" waltz and a Christmas Eve carol recitation with the whole family taking a turn. Her special-occasion poems gave all of us permission to try our hands at the arts without having to be perfect at any of them. The "Artist's Way" is about imperfection; about the great joy and freedom to be found in simply "practicing" a creative life. (Anything worth doing is worth doing badly, I like to joke.) I think of making love and making art as being very parallel. Even the most amateur attempt can be thrilling. Where does this leave the question of excellence? you may ask. Ours is a competitive, product-driven culture, and we have little experience with the notion of creative process for its own sake—The terror of being bad is often all that stands in the way of our being good. Being good may be a way station to excellence, but can be a lovely spot in and of itself. What we

seldom say is that creativity in and of itself is enjoyable—we are, all of us, far more creative than we dare hope if only we are willing to begin by being "yes, average". (1992, p. xii)

WHEN TO JOURNAL

When should journaling take place? Journaling can occur any time—in the classroom or in the field. Establish an expectation for two to three journaling exercises each day. State when and where this will happen in the agenda. Not to say this cannot be adjusted as need be, but putting it in writing sets the expectation. Additionally, encourage participants to write on their own time. Ask residence participants to always have their journal and a pencil at hand. To facilitate this we have found that furnishing a small journal satchel that can be carried over the shoulder when outdoors is extremely helpful.

Some environments seem especially conducive to reflective journaling: stream banks, overlooks with panoramic views, shady forests, sunny meadows, essentially any beautiful natural spot offering solitude and quiet. Even with a large group, a sense of solitude can be achieved when individuals are able to spread out a bit and find a comfortable spot that appeals to them. Sometimes the pace of a residential program or the energy level of participants will indicate when a journaling session might be beneficial.

SAMPLE ASSIGNMENTS

What follows is a selection of possible assignments. Choose the ones that seem most appropriate to setting and interests. Be aware of and follow regulations pertaining to the collection of natural objects. In some areas it is not appropriate or legal to pick plants. It is generally advisable to always return natural items to the areas in which they were found after observing them. This allows others to appreciate them, as well as for them to fulfill their subtle ecosystem roles. Provide a mix of writing and drawing exercises that help people focus on the environment, become fully present, engage the senses, exercise creativity, and become more self-aware. Begin journal entries by noting the physical location and date at the top of the page. Read selectively from journals of famous writers, artists, and others who have visited and written about this or a similar location. These can be inspirational to beginning journalists.

Include both directed journaling and time for open-ended writing each day. Briefly summarize experiences at day's end, inviting participants to share written pieces, photographs, or sketches.

Drawing any object forces us to look at it closely and see it more clearly. Many adults are fearful when asked to draw. Consider including a drawing class to help adults loosen up and lose some of their inhibition early in a class.

Back-to-Back Drawings is a fun way for people to lose inhibitions and get to know each other better. In an outdoor setting, ask each person to find a small natural object that can be concealed in the hand. This might be a pebble, stick, leaf, or a feather. They should try not to let others see what they select. Once all have found an object, instruct them to find a partner. Partners then sit on the ground back to back, and one at a time take turns providing verbal instructions to the other with the goal of having each person receiving the instructions accurately sketch the concealed item without seeing it or knowing what it is they are sketching. Objects should not be shown until the instructions/drawings are complete, and at no time during the description should the object be named.

Photography can effectively be incorporated into journals with some basic digital equipment and instruction. This is most effective when photography is combined with specific daily assignments and journaling questions and precede the actual taking of the photographs. For example, we have asked participants to focus on daily themes that have included wildlife, trees, and humans in the landscape. Some sample journal questions include the following, What comes to mind when considering the words wild/life? If trees could talk what might they say? Contemplate the human experience in this environment, past, present, and future. If photography is a primary focus, we provide up to four prints to each student per day to incorporate in their journals. Create brief "I-movies" each evening featuring the day's photographs and be sure to include some from all participants. These are very popular and allow critique and provide a powerful visual summary of the day.

Pick of the Pile is similar to Back-to-Back Drawing in that it encourages close attention to detail. Sitting in a circle, instruct each person to select one item from a pile of similar objects, such as leaves. Spend a few minutes writing detailed descriptions of the leaves on small pieces of paper. When finished, place the leaves back in the center of the circle. Fold papers and place in a hat. After mixing the papers, have each person select one, read it aloud, and attempt to match the written description with the correct leaf. When finished, discuss what made this task difficult or easy. Each person's leaf and matching description can then be taped into that person's journal.

Charcoal Drawings are novel when an actual piece of charcoal can be picked up from a burned area and used to sketch a landscape or a tree. This lends even an "average" drawing a powerful sense of authenticity!

Watercolors work similarly well, when water from a natural source is used for painting in the field. For example, paint the lake using water from the lake. This concept can be applied to streams, springs or puddles. Simple children's watercolor sets work fine, and are typically nontoxic. It is still advisable to empty dirty paint water away from the water source.

Georgia O'Keeffe Drawings are great fun wherever flowers bloom in profusion. Begin by sharing some of Georgia O'Keeffe's paintings of flowers. Once everyone has had the chance to admire some of her work, read to them the following quote:

A flower is relatively small. Everyone has many associations with a flower—the idea of flowers. You put out your hand to touch the flower—lean forward to smell it—maybe touch it with your lips almost without thinking—or give it to someone to please them. Still—in a way—nobody sees a flower really—it is so small—we haven't time—and to see takes time, like to have a friend takes time. If I could paint the flower exactly as I see it no one would see what I see because I would paint it small like the flower is small. So I said to myself—I'll paint what I see—what the flower is to me but I'll paint it big and they will be surprised into taking time to look at it—I will make even busy New Yorkers take time to see what I see of flowers. (Women in Art, n.d.)

Instruct participants to pick one flower to draw. They should begin by observing it very closely using a hand lens. They may want to imagine they are tiny ants, walking over every surface of the blossom. Once they have done this, they should make a sketch of the blossom, filling an entire journal page. Once the sketch is complete, have them add color to their drawings by using the pigments of the plant itself—simply pick the flower apart, then use fingers to rub the real petals onto the drawn petals, stem onto stem, leaves onto leaves.

Collections encourage exploration using the senses. We have used the headings "Yellowstone Sounds," "Yellowstone Smells," "Yellowstone Textures," "Yellowstone Colors" Substitute the residence location for Yellowstone. For more descriptive colors, suggest people make up new names for colors in the environment by adding a noun before the color. This might be as simple as "sky blue," but sometimes ends up as descriptively detailed as "sagebrush after afternoon downpour green" or "sleek September black bear brown." In *Pilgrim at Tinker Creek*, Annie Dillard said,

> I see what I expect. I once spent a full three minutes looking at a bullfrog that was so unexpectedly large I couldn't see it even though a dozen enthusiastic campers were shouting directions. Finally I asked, "What color am I looking for?" and a fellow said, "green." When at last I picked out the frog, I saw what painters are up against: the thing wasn't green at all, but the color of wet hickory bark. (1974, p. 20)

Another collection can be made by asking program participants to pick one color and put that color as a heading at the top of a page. Then, record everything seen during the residence that is a shade of that color.

Color to Describe Everything makes for strong and descriptive writing. At the end of a hike, or a day, ask participants to write answers to questions that sum up the experience, such as, "What color is the taste of rosehips?" "What color is the feel of Douglas fir bark?" "What color is the wind?" "What color is the smell of a campfire?" "What color are you in this environment?"

Paint Chips are the paper strips of color samples that can be found (and picked up for free!) where paint is sold. They are usually grouped by similar shades. Select in advance a diversity of paint chips representative of colors prevalent in the natural environment where the residence program is located. In geyser basins this includes pinks, yellows, oranges, browns, peaches, blues, creams, and grays. At a stop along the trail, just before entering an area such as a geyser basin, meadow, or riparian area, encourage close observation by giving each participant a strip and instructing them to find each shade on their strip between that point on the trail and the next stop. Allow them to quietly observe and meander through the area. Stop and ask them if they found all their colors. Did any surprise them?

Paint Strip Poetry can also be used as a simple framework for a poem. Ask participants to write a line in each color box. This should be a sentence or a phrase describing the environment they are in. The line should end with the color name printed at the bottom of the box. For example, if the box has the color name "eggshell" printed in it, a possible line might read, "We walked softly over pebbles the color of eggshell." Repeat for each color. When read together this makes for an interesting and sometimes humorous poem! Paint strips can be taped into journals with notation of date and place.

Facing Pages asks that residence participants open their journals to two facing blank pages. On the left side, have them spend two to five minutes recording everything around them: what they see, hear, smell, the temperature—the more detail the better. They should attempt to be "the scientist," recording observed data about the environment. Next, on the facing page, have them take the same amount of time to make observations, or collect data "from the inside"—recording everything they are feeling. Do this exercise often—in different environments and at different points in the course. This is also a good activity to repeat just prior to the wrap-up session. It helps people slow down and become more grounded physically and emotionally in where they are.

Acrostic Poetry stresses selecting a word relevant to the surroundings and spelling it vertically down the left margin of a page. Write a sentence or a phrase following each letter that begins with that letter.

Final Words is similar to an acrostic poem, but uses entire words positioned terminally in each line as a framework. Ask participants to think of eight words describing the environment they are in. These words should be written in a column vertically down the right side of a blank page. Looking at only one word at a time, participants should write a line ENDING in that word. Ask them not to look ahead. Instead they should look at one word, write the line, then move on to the next word and the next line. If the lines seem to fit together, fine. It is also okay to write each line as an individual thought.

Memory Maps are a great way to reflect on the events of a hike. Following a hike, ask participants to draw a map of the route in their journals from memory. They should add pictures and words as a record of experiences and thoughts encountered along the way.

Recipes are a fun way to think about details and incorporate them creatively into a description of a place. In this simple exercise, participants write a recipe for a place or an event. For example, they could write a recipe for a meadow, a canyon, or a thunderstorm.

Letters Home asks participants to write a letter to themselves. In the letter, they should describe adventures, experiences, thoughts. Ask them to include one thing they want to remember forever. These can be retained, then actually mailed to participants a month or so after the program has ended.

Searching is a good concluding exercise. People often come to wilderness areas searching for something but often do not know what it is until they find it. Invite participants to reflect and write about what they found during the time spent in wilderness that they needed. Finding the unexpected is part of the magic of wilderness.

EXAMPLES OF STUDENT WRITING

What follows are a few samples of journal entries, taken, with permission, from the journals of some of our residence participants.

Facing Pages

(August 22, 9:30 am, Bank of Rose Creek, Lamar, Yellowstone National Park)
I see, smell, hear . . .
Chilly. Prickly on my skin. Water cascading through the creek. Never ending, never changing. Black, cold ash in the fire pit. Damp with the morning dew. Sage, pine encompass me. Pebbles scattered about. Oval, round, but not regular. Circles. Constant, the bubbling creek. Clouds fill the morning sky. Sun gazing through gray curtains. Little warmth. Birds sing in the distance. A squirrel, too. Speaking to each other, answering, but in their native tongue. Green ribbons falling from the sky to touch my feet.
I feel . . .
I'm safe, yet vulnerable. Lonely, yet surrounded by the human consumption of the land. I'm restless, yet content. I am humbled to leave, but I want to stay. How the land touches my soul. Brings me into being. A new person yet the same. Different, but not. Landscapes that change over time. I influence this place just by being here. But it will continue after I'm gone.

Recipe for a Downpour

(July 17, Lamar Buffalo Ranch)
Strong breezes dashed with rain
Cottonwoods to blow
Wet sage
Wet earth

Strong clean smells
Heavy clouds in shades of gray
Evening light to make everything glow
Shirley with her hood up, wet face smiling
Proboscis
Laughter

Spread a rainbow over all. Share with a large number of friends from a covered back porch.

Yellowstone Colors

(September 19, Porcelain Basin, Norris Geyser Basin, Yellowstone National Park)
Sticky geranium purple
Yarrow leaf grey-green
Sulfur buckwheat yellow
Grizzly bear black
Black pool blue
Mimi's boots brown
Crested pool orange
Moon over Yellowstone Lake gold
Pelican Peak pink—evening shade

Yellowstone Sound Collection

(September 20, Upper Geyser Basin, Yellowstone National Park)
Elk bugling
Water and steam from mouth of Old Faithful
Guttural boom of Dragon's Mouth
Jay calling
Water entering Boiling River
Didgeridoo
Beautiful voices—Ron's, Susan's, Paul's. Others joining in.

Final Words

(September 19, Porcelain Basin, Norris Geyser Basin, Yellowstone National Park)

Shades of pastel apricot,	peach
Warm puffs of fragrant	steam
Breathe deep the Yellowstone	sulfur
Walk the steps of young	Kipling
Down the soft grey	boardwalk
Hear the sighs of unhappy	vent
Silent stands of bleached	lodgepole
Third week in	September

Yellowstone Magic

(Fall, Buffalo Ranch, Lamar, Yellowstone National Park)
 Hush, don't say a word,
But listen with your heart
To what this place would tell you
Of natures' work of art.
 The geysers' spouting water
Lifted upward to the sky,
*Will "kiss" you with its magic
And make you wonder why.*
 Just listen to the silence
That surrounds you like an arm
And you will hear the beauty
Of this place and all its charm.
 Then look into the night sky
Where the stars and moon reside
And feel the brilliant clearness
Of the Universe so wide.
 It's all a bit of magic
That Yellowstone does hold
And we are mighty lucky to see
Its wonders all unfold.
 Right before your very eyes

If you are quiet and serene
Yellowstone will open up
Nature's most magnificent scene.
      And you'll feel a bit of magic
As your heart within you swells
And you'll discover treasures
Where the wolf and bison dwell.
      The echoes of the present will
Mingle with the past
And time will cease to matter
As peace will come at last.
      You have to really look for it
This magic that is found
In wild and free places
Where nature does abound.
      Hold fast to this sweet magic
Take it with you when you go
In memories sweet and lasting
Of the land of the buffalo.

SUMMARY

This chapter defined journaling and discussed the benefits of journaling. It presented some specific suggestions for creating journals and facilitating journaling. Finally, we offered some sample assignments and shared examples of student writing. It is through journaling that program participants reflect upon the individual-wilderness relationship. Though some residence participants may initially resist this tool (as some resist sauntering), most develop an appreciation for the window journaling provides into the reflective process. In the final chapter we explore the overall value of adult residential education programs in wilderness areas.

CHAPTER 7

Final Thoughts

Prior to writing this book, we felt confident planning and conducting adult residential education programs in wilderness settings. We continue to be in awe of the transforming power of residence experiences and remain committed to creating programs that foster concern for all living things. But, writing this book brought home the complexity of these efforts. We are more thoughtful about how and more importantly why we design residence programs the way we do. We remain keenly aware of the vast wonders wilderness provides and how important wilderness may be to the emotional and physical well-being of humans. Opportunities to experience wilderness still exist, but there is continued pressure to develop these areas and make them more commercially useful. In the end, we recognize that the land is indeed a home that must be shared. It is also where great dramas still unfold and lessons abound for the patient observer.

In this book, we have attempted to introduce why we believe residential experiences for adults in wilderness settings are valuable. The need for such programs is multifaceted. In essence this includes the physical and emotional benefits wilderness conveys on humans and an imperative that humans gain greater understanding and take timely and decisive action to protect the earth's remaining wild lands. Thoreau's words sum it up quite succinctly, "In Wildness is the preservation of the World" (1862/1977, p. 609). This includes both the salvation of the physical planet as well as the salvation of the physical and emotional well-being of its human inhabitants. For educators, there is a pressing need to help navigate a way through the challenges posed by excessive consumption and overpopulation. Additionally, adult education professionals also need to explore and experiment with the most efficient and effective methods for teaching adults. Residential learning is a format that deserves wider use and continued experimentation to discover its maximal potential.

Toward this end, we have shared information from our own practice on how to successfully plan, execute, and conclude multiday, overnight wilderness experiences for adults. Our nuts-and-bolts treatment of the subject is by no means definitive; rather it is presented as a starting point. Future programs will continue to shape and redefine best practices. Readers are encouraged to share their own discoveries in contribution to the perfection of this craft.

Sauntering and journaling are two tools we find especially useful for helping participants more fully experience wilderness. Other methods of creative expression, such as photography, drawing, painting, music, dance, and play all hold great potential and deserve further exploration and treatment.

APPLYING LESSONS LEARNED

Perhaps of greatest interest and concern for adult education professionals is how these seemingly isolated experiences transfer "back home," for participants as well as for program planners. In other words, are the lessons learned and the principles applied to the design of adult residential education in wilderness areas restricted to the few days actually spent in residence or can they be more broadly applied? After participating in something so experiential, and after disconnecting from everyday responsibilities, how does one reconnect to everyday life?

Lessons for Participants

Over the years we have received a great deal of feedback from residence program participants and many attest to the transforming power of their experiences. They frequently comment on the content aspect of the program and share their enthusiasm for learning new information. They also acknowledge the overall effect of the residence itself, including the following as major benefits: enjoying more time outside; feeling more relaxed and a sharpening of their senses; being more fully cognizant of life lived in the present; reconnecting to the child within; and feeling a stronger connection to other life forms.

Enjoying Time Spent Outdoors

Perhaps the most common carryover from time spent in residence in wilderness is new or renewed valuing of time spent outdoors. Noted earlier, our programs are designed to encourage and support time spent outside. Whenever possible, programs and activities are structured to maximize time spent outdoors. In evaluations, participants frequently identify "time spent outside" as one of the most beneficial program elements and something they feel will have a lasting effect. Again and again participants assure us they are becoming better conditioned and will be able to hike more during the next program; they are walking more and spending more time simply enjoying being outdoors.

Heightening of the Senses and Feeling More Relaxed

We intentionally instruct participants on the value of relaxation and provide techniques for assisting them to monitor and regulate their bodies more consciously, to reduce tension, and to heighten feelings of well-being. At the same time, we provide participants with techniques to heighten their senses, to see more clearly, and to focus selectively, as well as to smell, hear, feel, and taste more intentionally and more fully. The first set of techniques is provided to relax the body; the second is provided to make the body more keenly sensitive to surroundings. While on the surface these two goals may appear contradictory, they are actually compatible and can be employed when participants return home.

Being More Fully Cognizant of the Present Moment

With heightened senses and relaxation strategies, participants can more fully experience the present. This is often a significant breakthrough for some program participants, initially accessible through the residence setting, but once experienced applicable elsewhere. By not having to attend to all the pressing demands surrounding daily life—responsibilities, for example, as parent, employee, and community member—residence participants relinquish countless burdens. Back home, allowing the senses to focus on the "now" can actually cleanse the mind, making it more alert and less lethargic.

Reconnecting to the Child Within

Perhaps one of the most lasting effects of a residence experience results from reconnecting to the child within. As Thoreau observed, within all adults endures the wild remnants of childhood. After time spent in residence, there is often increased sensitivity to the costs associated with civilizing forces. When adults are allowed to ignore many of the demands and responsibilities of daily living, allowed to live more fully in the present, allowed to play and to create, allowed to run and even to be silly, they tend to become more aware of the toll they pay daily to maintain membership in society. The big challenges facing participants once they return home are maintaining an attitude that values inquisitiveness, creativity, and playfulness, as well as holding on to the courage to forge new relationships.

Connecting to and Caring for Other Living Organisms

As mentioned earlier, community building is a significant component of our residence programs, but we view community much more broadly than encompassing only program participants. Therefore, we are very careful about how much emphasis is placed on group activities. Again, our major concern is not group cohesiveness, though it often emerges. We value attributes that strengthen the individual spirit—personal experiences, opportunity and tools for reflection, courage, awe, creativity, celebration of uniqueness, as well as acceptance and unconditional respect for others (other participants as well as other species). We are adamant about the nature of support individuals provide each other as well as all living things. We ask participants to care for the physical well-being of others, as well as themselves. One of the best results of a residence program is that participants often carry back to everyday life a bit more humility as human beings and a connectedness to a broader life community.

Lessons for Program Planners

Program planners are also participants in the experiences they create. Along with their clients, program planners often experience some sense of transformation as a result of their direct experience with planning and conducting a residence program. Whether changes are little or big, they are often significant. Program planners may feel hopeful and excited about holding onto these feelings once they return home—as well as fearful of losing them. Some may feel the need to share the experience with others who have not been involved in the program. Can their personal change endure beyond the residential setting? How is it possible to share their particular experience, that of both program planner and participant, with others? While not absolute, these things do at least seem possible. As noted above, program participants often discover new ways of relating and being, initially accessible through the wilderness residence setting. In some instances, these personal discoveries are so appealing, they transfer to old as well as to new environments, and when experimented with in a variety of settings and circumstances over time, prove so useful and effective as to become an enduring part of a new self-concept. This is also true for program planners. Resident planners continually influence and teach others, both wittingly and unwittingly through their own actions. Whenever positive traits are acquired, others benefit from the growth. Participants may in turn choose to adopt certain behaviors they see program planners modeling. This is the ultimate form of "sharing" a transformative learning experience.

A HINT OF MAGIC

In the preface we used the words *mysterious* and *magic* to describe what happens during residential programs in wilderness settings. What do we mean by "magic"? In Chapter 6 "Journaling" we included a poem by a participant titled "Yellowstone Magic". Bersch and Fleming (1997), in their analysis of residential programs said, "There remains just a hint of magic to learning in residence that defies certain description and that continues to set residential education apart" (p. 52). It is, indeed, not at all uncommon to hear the word *magic* used in reference to such programs. Yet it is a term that may make some people uncomfortable; it has made us as well as our students uncomfortable at times.

A class of University of Wyoming graduate students recently spent the months prior to one of our wilderness courses studying and discussing how planners construct such programs. In one class session, we discussed participant outcomes associated with the wilderness and residential format. In the weeks just prior to departure for the course, some students began experiencing a kind of performance anxiety—would their own experiences be magical or mundane? Program planners may wonder just how significant or huge their program impact will need to be to rate as "magical" for participants.

From our perspective, any time we experience or witness individual change and personal growth it seems magical. It need not, at first inspection, appear to be something huge. Indeed, change may often seem quite subtle and still prove significant over time. Another aspect that makes residential wilderness programs feel magical is their ability to surprise in terms of outcomes. Through our work, we have learned to expect the unexpected. Wildernesses have proven again and again to be incredibly rich treasure troves, beyond our wildest imaginings.

In Yellowstone, park managers continually search to understand the significance of the park and how to best care for it. When the park was established in 1872, it was set aside primarily for its unusual geology, such as its hot springs, mud pots, and geysers. Predecessors would have never suspected its significance today as a biosphere reserve and world heritage site. The large mammals visitors flock to the park to see today, such as elk, moose, and bears, were still fairly common across most of North America when the park was established. Early park promoters and enthusiasts would never have envisioned the significance of preserving the park microbes, let alone its clean air, natural quiet, or nighttime darkness. Today's visitors come to Yellowstone searching for all these things, and more. In *Searching for Yellowstone*, Paul Schullery said, "there are now so many searchers, and we have so many hopes, ambitions, and dreams for what we may find. And like our predecessors, we did not know until we found them that they were what we needed in the first place" (1999, p. 5).

Similarly, lessons learned through wilderness residences are not the same for each person. Instead each receives what is needed most. A child discovers he is able to eat something he did not think he liked. An unpopular child becomes well liked. Adults and children learn greater tolerance for others, including other life forms. One woman discovers how to be more fully present and engaged. A man is surprised to learn that others find him interesting. A few rediscover how good it makes them feel simply to be outside. Others are challenged physically and find they are able to do what they thought they could not. Some are reminded of how good it feels to laugh and to play and rediscover the joy of creativity without concern for product. Most leave appreciating wild lands, others, and themselves just a little bit more. Program planners are present at the most privileged, indeed, "magical" of moments!

IN CLOSING

We hope you find our ideas both helpful and provocative. May these pages provide the spark necessary to ignite the imagination to the potential such programs hold. If so, you may find the motivation to plan and deliver residential wilderness programs. The most important thing is simply to start doing it. Residence planners learn as they go. Rest assured, most successful adult education practitioners already know a lot about leading such programs! Program planners are alchemists. Mix together the right ingredients and a program is set in motion—an organic entity influenced by people and place, an organism that will take on a life of its own and evolve despite the best and worst of efforts. It is not all about leadership successes and failures. It is, however, up to individuals with vision to provide that crucial spark. Anatole France said,

> Do not try to satisfy your vanity by teaching a great many things. Awaken people's curiosity. It is enough to open minds; do not overload them. Put there just a spark. If there is some good inflammable stuff, it will catch fire. (Van Matre, 1983, p. 112)

May this book, in combination with the unique contributions of current and future adult education practitioners, produce a multitude of sparks. In due time, may it produce a conflagration of good, for the earth and all its inhabitants.

We close with one final observation by Paul Schullery, an observation made in a PBS video produced in 2000, *The Living Edens: Yellowstone, America's Sacred Wilderness*. Though he is discussing the mysterious effect Yellowstone has on people, his remarks can certainly be applied to wilderness in general and to relationships still to be formed:

> There are very few places left in the world where you can watch wild nature express itself. And for reasons that I can't fully explain or articulate, that has an almost magical power. When we witness the drama of this wilderness [Yellowstone], it is obvious that there is a relationship between the predators and the prey and between the plants and the animals. But where does that leave us? I'm afraid that most people still don't think of themselves as having a relationship with nature. They think of nature as something that happens somewhere out there, in some remote place like Yellowstone, and they feel completely isolated from it. But unless we're aware of how deeply we're connected to nature, and how intimate that connection is, we're in big trouble; because we can't afford to treat nature badly. Saving elk and wolves and saving places like Yellowstone shouldn't be an excuse for mistreating nature anywhere else. These days I hear a lot of

people asking if we can protect wildness in Yellowstone. But I don't think that's the question at all. The wolves and [the] mountain lions have shown us that even lost wildness can be restored. Whether we do it ourselves or let nature do it for us, we can save wild nature wherever we want to. I think the question is "Do we have the courage to do it?" We know how. The great peril that Yellowstone faces is the failure of human courage.

APPENDIX A

Program Description

Here is a basic description of an adult residential education program offered in Yellowstone National Park in August 2005. It is a preliminary advertisement, appearing nine months prior to the event. The complete description includes information about the sponsoring institution, a registration form, artwork, and contact information.

Home on the Range: Habitat Selection in Yellowstone's Lamar Valley August 15–20, 2005

Yellowstone habitat and the wildlife it supports are the focus of this five-night residential learning program. Through this program, participants gain a comprehensive understanding of habitat as a way to better understand wildlife presence and behavior. Why humans feel good in certain environments and prefer specific habitats is also explored.

Content goals are achieved through direct exploration of the area's wild ridges, rivers, lakes, forests, and meadows. This is an active course with at least half of each day spent outside. Activites include moderate hikes of approximately one to five miles each day, with less active and more active options available.

While we spend much time engaged in formal learning, each day also includes opportunities to interact informally with others as well as time for personal reflection. Journaling is an integral part of this course. Residential learning in wilderness settings provides adults with unique opportunities for renewal and growth. Physically and emotionally removed from everyday roles, responsibilities, and pressures, a child-like sense of freedom results—freedom to form new relationships, discuss ideas, create, reflect, and play. We attempt to honor and facilitate learning in all its forms.

Peaceful and spectacular home to wolves, bears, elk, and bison, the Lamar Valley is an ideal setting for learning. The historic Lamar Buffalo Ranch facility includes simple and comfortable accommodations in log guest cabins, a heated bathhouse with showers and restrooms, and a common building with classrooms and kitchen. Guests are expected to bring a sleeping bag and pillow. Meals are provided. Participants share space in cabins that include three single beds, a propane heater, and reading lights. The cabins do not have electrical outlets or plumbing.

Ellen Petrick, M.S.—Educational Consultant, will be the lead instructor for this course. Ellen has worked in informal education for over 20 years. For eight years Ellen served as Education Program Manager for the National Park Service in Yellowstone National Park. This is her fourth collaboration with the University of Wyoming.

The cost of the program is $500. This fee covers the cost of instruction, lodging, transportation inside the park, meals, and park entrance. Registration is on a first come, first served basis and the course is expected to fill quickly. A deposit of $250 is required within two weeks of registration. The additional $250 is due no later than July 15, 2005.

APPENDIX B

Program Packet

Included here are samples of some of the materials sent to participants approximately two months prior to a residence program in 2004: *Lamar Landscapes: Focusing on Our Wild Nature.* The packet includes a welcome letter, agenda, and clothing and equipment list.

WELCOME LETTER

The intent of the welcome letter is to establish a tone of anticipation, and to set some expectations—for us as well as for the participants. Information on recommended reading and other preparation is enclosed.

Dear Registered Participant,

Welcome to "Lamar Landscapes: Focusing on Our Wild Nature," sponsored by the University of Wyoming's Department of Adult Learning and Technology. This four night residential learning experience will occur in Yellowstone National Park August 18–22, 2004 at the historic Lamar Buffalo Ranch Field Campus in the Lamar Valley. Peaceful and spectacular home to wolves, bears, elk, and bison, Lamar Valley is an excellent place to experience and learn about Yellowstone.

Participants will gain an intimate sense of place through experiencing the valley's geologic past, human stories, and abundance of life forms. Course content will be presented through a diversity of classroom and field sessions, with primary emphasis on being out in the resource. The physical experience of simply being in a place of astounding natural beauty can profoundly influence our psyches. Why we feel good in certain environments will be explored from the perspectives of personal experience and sociobiology.

Through a dynamic blending of simple writing and photographic exercises, participants will become keen observers of both external and internal landscapes: What we see and how it makes us feel. Course journals will serve as a tool to capture these dual observations. Participants will create beautiful hand-stitched books to chronicle their own personal journey during the course. Images of wildlife and nature by painters and photographers such as Thomas Moran, Lanford Monroe, J. K. Hillers, and Jim Brandenburg will heighten our appreciation and serve as inspiration in the creation of our own photographic and sketchbook images.

Ellen Petrick-Underwood, M.S. -Educational Consultant, will be the lead instructor for this course. Ellen has worked in informal education for 20 years. For eight years Ellen served as Education Program Manager for the National Park Service in Yellowstone National Park. National Museum of Wildlife Art Curator of Education Jane Lavino has 20 years of experience in art education. Jane will lead the art discussions and art-making sections of the program. Ellen and Jane are identical triplet sisters. This is the first class they will teach together. Rounding out the instructor team will be Norm Bishop—International Wolf Center field representative for the greater Yellowstone region. Norm enjoyed a 36-year career with the National Park Service, the last 17 at Yellowstone where he was instrumental in paving the way for wolf restoration. Norm will lead the wolf sessions.

Check-in will be between 5:00 and 7:00 PM on August 18 at the Lamar Buffalo Ranch (Yellowstone Association Institute). Please plan on having dinner on your own prior to 7:00 PM, either on your way into the park, or in the vicinity of the Buffalo Ranch following check-in. The campus is located in the northeast portion of the park on the road between Roosevelt and Cooke City, Montana. The Lamar Buffalo Ranch Field Campus provides simple, yet comfortable accommodations in log guest cabins. There is a heated bathhouse with showers and restrooms, and a common building with classrooms and kitchen.

Students are expected to bring a sleeping bag and pillow (please refer to the "Clothing and Equipment List" for more details). Meals will be provided. Participants share space in cabins that include three single beds, a propane heater, and reading lights. The cabins do not have electrical outlets or plumbing. Once in the park, you will travel in Institute vans. Days will be long and full. The course itinerary is included for your review. While we have attempted to provide a variety of activities, five days is simply not enough! You may choose to extend your trip to include other park areas that we will not have time to visit as a group. The sheer size (2.2 million acres) and wealth of Yellowstone's resources is truly astounding.

Meals during the course (with the exception of dinner the first night) will be provided by caterers Ron and Susan Mavrich of Laramie. See the agenda for their menu. We are so lucky Ron and Susan are willing to travel to cook for us and share their musical talent! Please let us know as soon as possible if you are vegetarian or have other dietary restrictions, and we will plan accordingly.

Park entrance fees are waived for course participants. You will need to show your pass (this will be mailed) at the entrance gate upon arrival, so don't forget to bring it with you!

We look forward to sharing our long fascination and delight in this place with you! See you in August.

If you have any questions, please don't hesitate to contact Ellen directly.

Sincerely,
Ellen, Jane, and Norm

Recommended Texts

There are two highly recommended books for course participants. The first is *Resources and Issues 2004*. This book is produced in-house as a training manual for park naturalists and is updated each year. It is available (though not until June) through the Yellowstone Association's mail sales for approximately $13.95. The second is *Searching For Yellowstone*, by Paul Schullery, First Mariner Books, Houghton Mifflin Co., 1997. All proceeds from the sale of these books go directly back into Yellowstone National Park. To order by mail call toll free at 1–877–967–0090. It would be helpful to read as much as possible before the class, and bring both books with you when you come to the park.

Other Preparation

Any additional reading you can do on Yellowstone will be beneficial, and a wealth of material is available. Try your local library. Books are also available through the Yellowstone Association. The National Park Service web site is another excellent source of park information. Find it at *www.nps.gov/yell*. To get to the expanded site, click on "inDEPTH." The site includes a series of electronic field trips. While these were designed for middle school audiences, they provide excellent background material on wolves, bears, and other wildlife and related park topics. Online tours are a good way to get a glimpse of some of the landscapes you will be visiting. This is an active program. Any walking or hiking you do in preparation will be beneficial.

AGENDA

What follows is the agenda for a four-day program we offered in Yellowstone National Park in 2004: *Lamar Landscapes: Focusing on Our Wild Nature*

Wednesday, August 18—Arrival/Orientation   Start 7:00 PM

5:00–7:00 PM   Arrival and check-in at Buffalo Ranch, move into cabins (please plan on having dinner on your own prior to 7:00 PM, either on your way

	into the park, or in the vicinity of the Buffalo Ranch following check-in).
7:00 PM	Meet in the Lamar Bunkhouse: course overview, group introductions/activities.
7:40 PM	"Now That You're Here—", What is unique about residential experiences in wilderness areas?—A theoretical and practical discussion of likely and possible outcomes from your program planners (Michael and Ellen)
8:00 PM	Evening walk. Slow down and open the senses. Overview of geology, wildlife and history of the area.
9:00PM	Campfire

Thursday August 19—Focus on Wildlife   Start 8:30 AM

7:30 AM	Breakfast: Breakfast burrito w/salsa; fresh fruit; juice/coffee/hot tea
8:30 AM	Understanding Connection to Place: Why Does it Feel Good Here? (Ellen)
9:15 AM	The Art of Photography—slide talk; Project Introduction (Jane)
10:15 AM	Orientation to digital cameras—how to use them and logistics of sharing them (John)
10:45 AM	Creation of books/Creative exercises (Jane and Ellen)
12:00 noon	Sack Lunch: Italian focaccia sandwich; German potato salad; carrot/celery; apple, cookie
1:00 PM	Wolf Tales—Participative readings about wolf encounters (Norm)
2:00 PM	More Active Option (Norm) Hike to historic Rose Creek pen site where Norm will share his personal experiences with wolf restoration. This hike is approximately 2 mile round trip and has a 500 foot elevation gain.
	Less Active Option (Ellen) For those desiring a less active option, join Ellen in the Lamar Bunkhouse where she will share her personal

reflections on wolf reintroduction and show a recent wolf video.

4:00 PM   Break

5:00 PM   Yellowstone Wolves—Wolf Restoration slide talk (Norm)
               We'll learn how and why wolves were restored to Yellowstone as an experimental population under the Endangered Species Act. Find out what wolves eat, how they kill their prey, and what effect wolves have on other animals, including livestock outside the park.

6:00 PM   Dinner: Sun dried tomato pesto chicken; pasta; salad; bread; dessert; iced tea

7:00 PM   Northern Range slide talk (Lamar Bunkhouse)
               Norm will share fact and fiction surrounding one of the park's longest running and most controversial management issues—and in what ways recent research indicates wolves are altering the picture.

Friday, August 20—Focus on Wolves,
Petrified Trees   **Start 6:00 AM**

6:00 AM   Sack breakfast on the road: Granola; cinnamon raisin scones; fresh fruit; juice/coffee/hot tea
               Practice patience not far from the roadside watching for wolves and other wildlife. Be prepared to do some walking and climb several hundred feet up steep slopes. Length of time in the field will depend on wolf visibility.

TBA   Meet at the Lamar Bunkhouse for a brief overview of park geology using simple models and a timeline demonstration. (Time TBA, based on wolf activity)
               Sack Lunch: Turkey cranberry wrap; Southwest cole slaw; chips; apple; cookie

Afternoon   More Active Option (Ellen) Specimen Ridge Hike. This is a steep, strenuous hike. Three miles round trip (4.8 km). Elevation gain of

1200 feet in 1.5 miles. This trail leads to a few of the most impressive petrified trees, with commanding views of the Lamar River, Slough Creek, and the surrounding mountain ranges. If time allows, join the rest of the group on the porch of the Roosevelt Lodge before heading back to the ranch for dinner.

Less Active Option (Jane) View the Petrified Tree on the Mammoth-Tower road (accessible by car). Drive to Tower Fall (132 feet). View falls from the overlook (100 yards from parking) or walk to the bottom (0.5 mi., 200 foot descent). End the day on the porch of the Roosevelt Lodge, with conversation and refreshment. Some may also choose to take the short hike behind the lodge to Lost Creek Falls (0.2 mi.). Continuing on to Lost Lake is a 2 mile (3.2 km) round trip distance from the lodge.

7:00 PM	Dinner: Green chili taco lasagna: salad with honey chili dressing; cornbread; dessert; iced tea
8:00 PM	Photo Review in the Lamar Bunkhouse (Jane) Following this session (approx. 30–45 minutes), a selection of videos will be available for viewing (optional).

Saturday, August 21—Focus on the Human Experience   Start 8:30 AM

7:30 AM	Breakfast: Egg casserole; biscuits; fresh fruit; juice/coffee/hot tea
8:30 AM	Hike to a cultural site in Lamar Valley. Contemplate the human experience here through time: Sheepeaters and other tribes of native peoples, mountain men, miners, explorers, artists, cavalry, rangers, winter enthusiasts, and wolf watchers—
Sack Lunch:	Turkey pesto sandwich; Mediterranean pasta salad; carrot/celery; apple; cookie

Afternoon: More Active Option (Jane) Upper Meadows of Pebble Creek: 4 miles round trip (out and back trail). This hike is a steep climb but well worth the effort. You ascend to a high, secluded glacial valley, the upper meadows of Pebble Creek, amid some of the park's tallest peaks. Trail climbs 1000 feet in 1.5 miles, then descends 200 feet to the meadows and banks of Pebble Creek. Excellent views of Barronette Peak and Abiathar Peak.
Less Active Option (Ellen): Drive to the northeast entrance, stopping to look for mountain goats on Barronette Peak. Experience Cooke City's unique charm—dramatic peaks, a general store, homemade pie, and more.

7:00 PM   Dinner: Rosemary and cranberry roast pork loin; scalloped potatoes; salad; bread; dessert; iced tea
8:00 PM   Work on Journals—integration of photos (Lamar Bunkhouse)
9:00 PM   Final Campfire with Ron, Susan, and all of us.

Sunday, August 22—Conclusion

7:30 AM   Breakfast: Granola/bread/fruit
8:00–9:00 AM   Clean-up, pack up, load vehicles.
9:00 AM   Time for final reflections/sharing/good-byes at campfire circle
Dismissal by 10:00 AM

CLOTHING AND EQUIPMENT LIST

What follows are a brief message and a listing and clothing and equipment suggestions shared with participants a few months before the program begins. We basically follow the listing provided by the Yellowstone Institute to their program participants (the listing is used with the permission of the Yellowstone Institute). We also include a listing of what to bring if the residence is being held in a dormitory or a cabin and also what toiletries to bring based upon characteristics of the bathhouse.

General Clothing and Equipment

Because much class time will be spent outdoors and all courses are held rain or shine, program participants should be prepared for a variety of mountain weather conditions, including cold temperatures. You are encouraged to wear synthetic and wool clothing and to generally avoid wearing anything cotton (the fabric maintains moisture, gets heavy when wet, and is a major chill producer). As for appropriate equipment, from hiking shoes to backpacks, our major advice is to try them before coming to the residence and only to bring what has been found comfortable and useful. Appropriate rain gear, clothing, and footwear are very important. Here are some clothing and equipment suggestions:

Clothing

_____ Socks
_____ Hiking boots
_____ Spare pair of shoes
_____ Thermal underwear (tops and bottoms)
_____ Short sleeve shirt
_____ Long sleeve shirt (light and heavy)
_____ Sweater or sweatshirt (wool or polartec/fleece-type)
_____ Long pants
_____ Shorts
_____ Light coat and/or windbreaker
_____ Warm coat
_____ Rain gear (top for sure and bottoms if you have them)
_____ Hat (a warm one and one for the sun)
_____ Gloves/mittens

Miscellaneous
_____ Day pack
_____ Water bottle (with tight fitting screw lid)
_____ Sunglasses and sunscreen
_____ Lip balm
_____ Pocketknife
_____ Reading material
_____ Insect repellant
_____ Earplugs (roommates may snore)

Cabins Sleeping Areas
_____ Sleeping bag
_____ Pillow
_____ Extra blanket
_____ Non-electric alarm clock
_____ Flashlight

Bathroom Facilities
_____ Towel and wash cloth
_____ Toiletries

Course Equipment List
Journals: For this course we will provide each participant with materials to create your own creative journal
(to include writing and photography). Throughout the
course you will make entries through guided activities as
well as independent writing and sketching.
Pencils: Please bring at least two number 2 or HB hard-
ness pencils. Pencils work better than pens in some
weather conditions, and you may want to use them for
sketching.
Camera: If possible bring a camera and film; digital cam-
eras also encouraged. (May be required for certain
classes.)
Field Guides: Bring any you like that are appropriate for
the area, but you do not need to buy them for the course.
Binoculars and spotting scopes: Bring them if you have
them. Spotting scopes will be provided for wildlife
watching.

APPENDIX C

Program Evaluation

Below is the program evaluation form used for a residence program in 2004. To be included in this publication, spacing has been modified. Omitted is the title, sponsor, and location of the program, instructor names, and return mailing information.

EVALUATION FORM

Please take a few moments to complete this evaluation while impressions are still fresh. Evaluations are due back by September 20, 2004. Return this form to—Your comments will help us plan similar classes in the future. Thank you!

1. How did you learn about this program?
2. Why did you decide to participate?
3. What was most memorable about this program?
4. What would you tell a friend about this program?
5. Our primary goals in conducting these programs are to promote stewardship of natural areas, and to promote personal renewal and growth. We attempt to achieve these goals through facilitating connections with the land and with people in an immersion environment. In what ways did you benefit from this approach?
6. Please consider the following possible outcomes, then rank each statement on a scale of one to five, where **1 means you strongly agree** with the statement, **5 means you strongly disagree** with the statement. Please circle a number to correspond with each statement.

	Strongly Agree			Strongly Disagree		Not Applicable
a. This program helped me acquire and use new information.	1	2	3	4	5	N/A
b. This program helped me make new friends, develop new contacts, or share ideas with family, friends, or coworkers.	1	2	3	4	5	N/A
c. This program helped me gain a deeper appreciation of the arts and/or sciences.	1	2	3	4	5	N/A
d. This program helped me gain a deeper sense of connection and responsibility toward the natural world.	1	2	3	4	5	N/A
e. This program helped me feel more self-aware or self-confident.	1	2	3	4	5	N/A
f. This program helped me feel more appreciative or tolerant of others.	1	2	3	4	5	N/A
g. This program gave me a sense of renewal. It made me feel more relaxed, in touch with the present, creative and playful.	1	2	3	4	5	N/A
h. This program caused me to reexamine my ideas about how the world works, or fundamentally changed my understanding of the world.	1	2	3	4	5	N/A

7. Please evaluate the effectiveness of your instructors by offering suggestions to each so that he or she may improve their instruction.

8. Is there anything about the class you would have changed? If yes, what?

9. Do you have any ideas for future programs?

Thank you for taking the time to complete this evaluation. Feel free to include any other comments on additional sheets of paper. Return this form to . . .

REFERENCES

Andy Goldsworthy Art Links. (n.d.). Retrieved June 15, 2005, from http://www.artcyclopedia.com/artists/goldsworthy andy.html

Bersch, G., & Fleming, J. A. (1997). Residential workshops. *New Directions for Adult and Continuing Education, 76,* 51–58.

Brock, T. D. (1994). *Life at high temperatures.* Yellowstone National Park: Yellowstone Association for Natural Science, History & Education.

Caffarella, R. S. (2002). *Planning programs for adult learners: A practical guide for educators, trainers, and staff developers,* 2nd Ed. San Francisco: Jossey-Bass.

Cameron, J. (1992). *The artist's way.* New York: Putnam.

Cameron, J. (1996). *The vein of gold.* New York: Putnam.

Campbell, C. (1994). *The backpacker's photography handbook.* New York: Amphoto Books.

Carson, R. (1956). *The sense of wonder.* New York: Harper & Row.

Craze, R. (2001). *Alexander Technique.* Lincolnwood, IL: Contemporary Books.

Day, M. (1981). *Adult education as a new educational frontier: Review of the Journal of Adult Education 1929–1941.* Unpublished doctoral dissertation, University of Michigan, Ann Arbor.

Dewey, J. (1963). *Experience and education.* New York: Collier. (Original work published 1938)

Dillard, A. (1974). *Pilgrim at Tinker Creek.* New York: HarperCollins.

Dillard, A. (1982). *Teaching a stone to talk.* New York: Harper & Row.

Durrell, G. (1982). *The amateur naturalist.* New York: Alfred A. Knopf.

Faculty of Harvard Medical School (2004). Consumer health information. Retrieved June 15, 2005, from http://www.intelihealth.com/IH/ihtIH/WSIHW000/408/408.html

Ferra, L. (1994). *A crow doesn't need a shadow: A guide to writing poetry from nature.* Salt Lake City: Peregrine Smith Books.

Fitzharris, T. (2003). *National Audubon Society guide to nature photography, Revised Edition.* Buffalo, NY: Firefly Books.

Fleming, J. A. (1996). *Participant perceptions of residential learning.* Unpublished doctoral dissertation, University of Northern Colorado, Greeley.

Fleming, J. A. (1997). The power of detachment and continuity. *Adult Education Quarterly, 48* (4), 260–272.

Fleming, J. A. (1998). *How learning in residence fosters transformative learning and connected teaching.* Paper presented at the Midwest Research-to-Practice Conference in Adult, Continuing and Community Education, Michigan State University. http://www.anrecs.msu.edu/research/fleming.htm

Geisel, T. (1986). *You're only old once!: A book for obsolete children.* New York: Random House.

Harding, W. (1992). *The days of Henry David Thoreau: A biography.* Princeton, NJ: Princeton University Press.

Hart, J. (1998). *Walking softly in the wilderness: The Sierra Club guide to backpacking.* San Francisco: Sierra Club Books.

Hinchman, H. (1991). *A life in hand: Creating the illuminated journal.* Layton, UT: Dibbs Smith.

Hinchman, H. (1997). *A trail through leaves: The journal as a path to place.* New York: W. W. Norton.

Houle, C. O. (1971). *Residential continuing education.* Syracuse University: Publication in Continuing Education.

Knowles, M. (1977). *A history of the adult education movement in the United States.* Huntington, NY: Robert E. Krieger Publishing. (Original work published 1962)

Knox, A. (1981). Adults as learners. *Museum News, 59,* (5).

Leave No Trace: Center for Outdoor Ethics. (n.d.) Home page. Retrieved June 15, 2005, from http://www.LNT.org/main.html; 1-800-332-4100.

Lee, W. (1996). *A guide to photographing Rocky Mountain wildlife.* Englewood, CO: Westcliffe Publishers.

Leopold, A. (1968). *Sand County almanac and sketches here and there.* Oxford: Oxford University Press. (A Sand County Almanac originally published 1949)

The Leopold Institute perspective. (n.d.). Retrieved June 15, 2005, from http://leopold.wilderness.net/aboutus/whatisw.htm

Lindeman, E. C. (1989). *The meaning of adult education.* Norman, Oklahoma: Oklahoma Research Center for Continuing Professional and Higher Education. (Original work published 1926)

Martin, E. D. (1926). *The meaning of a liberal education*. Chicago: American Library Association.

Merriam, S. B., & Brockett, R. G. (1997). *The profession and practice of adult education: An introduction*. San Francisco: Jossey-Bass.

Nash, R. (2000). *Wilderness and the American mind*, 4th Ed. New Haven and London: Yale University Press.

National Committee on Science Education Standards and Assessment, National Research Council. (1995). *National science education standards*. Washington DC: The National Academies Press.

National Outdoor Leadership School Wilderness Medicine Institute. (n.d.). Retrieved June 15, 2005, from http://www.wmi.net.au/wmi/

Ohliger, J. (2001). Does adult education exist? In M. Day (Ed.), *Proceedings from the Jackson Hole Symposium on Graduate Study in Adult Education and Instructional Technology* (pp. 13–17). Laramie, WY: University of Wyoming.

Oliver, M. (1992). *New and selected poems*. Boston: Beacon Press.

Patton, M. Q. (1997). *Utilization-focused evaluation*, 3rd Ed. Thousands Oaks, CA: SAGE Publications.

Project Wild Activity Guide. (1992). Bethesda, MD: Western Regional Environmental Education Council, Inc.

Pine, J. (1999, November 15). Interview: B. Joseph Pine—Experience Required. *CIO Magazine*.

Roethke, T. (1966). *Roethke: Collected poems*. New York: Doubleday. (Original work published 1953)

Sachatello-Sawyer, B., Fellenz, R., Burton, H., Gittings-Carlson, L., Lewis-Mahony, J., Woolbaugh, W. (2002). *Adult museum programs: Designing meaningful experiences*. Walnut Creek, CA: AltaMira Press.

Schullery, P. (2000). *The living Edens: Yellowstone, America's sacred wilderness*. ABC/Kane Productions International: PBS Home Video.

Schullery, P. (1988). *Mountain time: Man meets wilderness in Yellowstone*. New York: Simon & Schuster.

Schullery, P. (1999). *Searching for Yellowstone: Ecology and wonder in the last wilderness*. Boston: Houghton Mifflin.

Scriven, M. (1994). Using student ratings in teacher evaluation. *Evaluation Perspectives*, 4 (1).

Shaw, J. (2000). *Nature photography field guide*. New York: Amphoto Books.

Thoreau, H. D. (1977). A week on the Concord and Merrimack Rivers. In C. Bode (Ed.), *The portable Thoreau* (pp. 138–227). New York: Penguin. (Original work published 1849)

Thoreau, H. D. (1977). Walking. In C. Bode (Ed.), *The portable Thoreau* (pp. 592–630). New York: Penguin. (Original work published 1862)

Thoreau, H. D. (1985). *Walden.* New York: The Library of America. (Original work published 1854)

Tilden, F. (1977). *Interpreting our heritage.* Chapel Hill: University of North Carolina Press. (Original work published 1957)

The United States Federal Wilderness Act of 1964. (1964). Public Law 88-577, 88th Congress, S.4, September 3, 1964.

Van Matre, S. (Ed.). (1983). *The earth speaks.* Greenville, WV: The Institute for Earth Education.

Whitney, S. (1997). *Western forests.* New York: Alfred A. Knopf.

The Wilderness Society. (n.d.). Retrieved June 15, 2005, from http://www.wilderness.org/

Wilson, E. O. (1984). *Biophilia.* Cambridge: Harvard University Press.

Wilson, E. O. (2002). *The future of life.* New York: Vintage Books.

Wiltz, K. (2001). *Proceedings of the Teton summit for program evaluation in nonformal education.* Unpublished proceedings distributed by The Ohio State University, Department of Program Development and Evaluation.

Wlodkowski, R. J. (1999). *Enhancing adult motivation to learn: A comprehensive guide for teaching all adults.* San Francisco: Jossey-Bass.

Women in Art. Georgia O'Keeffe (1887–1986). (n.d.). Retrieved June 15, 2005, from http:/www.mystudios.com/women/klmno/okeefe.html

Wordsworth, W. (1932). *The complete poetical works of Wordsworth.* Boston: Houghton, Mifflin and Co. (Original poem penned 1807)

World Health Organization (1948). WHO Definition of health. Retrieved June 15, 2005, from http://www.who.int/about/definition/en/

INDEX